Legacy

John Gibb

Legacy

The Changing Face of the Landscape

Foreword	MARCUS BINNEY
Photographs	CLIVE ARROWSMITH
	DERRY BRABBS
	HARRY DE ZITTER
	BRIAN HARRIS
	BARRY LATEGAN
	DAN LEPARD
	PATRICK LICHFIELD
	LINDA McCARTNEY
	TONY McGEE
	NORMAN PARKINSON
	MARTIN TRELAWNY
	DENIS WAUGH

JONATHAN CAPE
LONDON

To Rosemary
and Eloise

J G

First published 1990
© CPRE 1990

Jonathan Cape Ltd, 20 Vauxhall Bridge Road, London SW1V 2SA

A CIP catalogue record for this book
is available from the British Library

ISBN 0–224–02681–X

Designed by Peter Guy
Phototypeset by Keyspools Ltd, Warrington
Printed in Italy by
Arti Grafiche Motta S.p.A.-Milan

Contents

Acknowledgments

CPRE would like to express its deep gratitude to Shell UK without whose sponsorship the entire Legacy project including this book would not have been possible, and would also like to thank the Countryside Commission, Dr Sadie Ward and Dr Jonathan Brown of the Institute of Agricultural History at Reading University, Protocol and, above all, the photographers featured in this book, who gave their time and skills to CPRE for love of the countryside

Foreword

by Marcus Binney

THE ENGLISH LANDSCAPE is mankind's supreme contribution to the beauty of this planet. Other countries, other continents, other islands may boast more majestic mountains, mightier rivers, lovelier lakes, but nowhere else has the hand of man wrought such an intricate and varied picture as in England. Generation after generation has not simply sought to improve and exploit the land, but has cared deeply for its look and ambience – and has always planted for the future as well as the present.

The Council for the Protection of Rural England was born of a mounting anger that this accumulation of beauty and character would be dissipated within a few decades by both sprawling development and thoughtless disfiguration of fine scenery. This book is a record of great victories and tragic waste – and of battles that never cease.

Some parts of the country have substantially retained their special character while others have entirely lost them. The message which shines through these pages is that those places which have kept their character are not simply cosy little countryside inglenooks where the clock has been made artificially to stand still. They are just as likely to be the seat of prosperous farming and successful woodland management.

Fly into London's Heathrow airport and your plane descends across some of the best horticultural land in Europe – entirely submerged in suburbia. Circle above Gatwick, however, and you will see a pattern of irregular fields embedded in virtual woodland. These strips of wood, known as shaws, were left as shelter by the Sussex farmers who opened up the fields in the twelfth and thirteenth centuries. The land form has changed little in seven hundred years.

Drive across the Vale of Belvoir and you will find one of the most magical landscapes in England – mile after mile of well-tended hedges, plenty of hedgerow trees, and hardly an ugly modern farm building to be seen. Leave the Vale and suddenly you may be in a featureless prairie.

Looking at some of the photographs in this book it is often hard not to conclude that the planners of motorways, new towns and nuclear power stations simply take a ruler and seek out those areas which are furthest away from centres of population – and potential local opposition. But in doing this they inevitably select the very places it is most essential to protect.

The origin of this book lies in the discovery by John Gibb of a vast and virtually unknown photographic archive at the Institute of Agricultural History at Reading University. In addition early photographs were unearthed from filing cabinets in dusty provincial newspaper offices, and from CPRE's own collections at Reading, to which many amateur photographers have bequeathed their stock.

Following this, CPRE embarked on the Legacy project, inviting photographers to go out into today's countryside and make a comparative record that conveys the essence of change, survival and threat. The importance of this book is that it combines very personal photography with a deliberately documentary approach. The aim is not simply to produce a photograph that is a work of art, or a pretty or memorable picture, but one that makes a clear statement about the condition of the landscape, ravishing or ravaged. And it is here that the skill of the Legacy photographers is most evident.

It is a relatively easy matter to work out how to photograph a building to most telling advantage, even if distant views have to be sought out for the first time. It takes much longer to find and assess the best viewpoints of a larger landscape. Waiting for the right light may take longer still, especially in winter months when weather may be flat and grey over four or five weeks. A great decaying country house, or a bird suffering due to an oil slick, is immediately poignant. Damage to the countryside is much more difficult to convey graphically. A majestic sweep of Down that has been ploughed for prairie farming – destroying age-old pasture and all the evidence of man's continuous occupation it contained – can still make a beautiful photograph. The camera, presented with a panorama of golden corn, or freshly ploughed furrows continuing to the horizon, too easily produces an image where starkness is transformed into an attractive sim-

plicity, conflicting with a caption which states that this is a landscape shorn of history, character and charm.

In this book CPRE has found a powerful new way of proclaiming its message and telling its story. Much of CPRE's success over the sixty-plus years charted here has been due to its willingness to go on the offensive. A voluntary organisation involved with the environment can easily spend its whole time responding to threats and proposals of different kinds. Such monitoring is vital. But sometimes a much bigger breakthrough can be made by challenging the basis on which the Government is taking decisions, and by pinpointing new directions Government policy can take. This has been the hallmark of CPRE over the last six and a half decades.

The rollcall of its campaigns makes impressive reading and gives a real insight into its preoccupations and challenges. The national joint committee to preserve the countryside was formed in December 1926 as the Council for the Preservation of Rural England (Preservation was later changed to Protection). A year later its first annual report announced an all-out attack on ribbon development. In 1929 CPRE wrote to the Prime Minister urging the case for National Parks. The Ribbon Development Act in 1935 crowned the then nine-year-long CPRE campaign. The next year witnessed the historic agreement between CPRE and the Forestry Commission protecting the central fells of the Lake District from afforestation. CPRE joined with the National Trust and the Commons Society in 1937 to turn a national spotlight on coastal despoliation.

CPRE was again campaigning for National Parks in 1946 and was suggesting comprehensive planning legislation; three years later it was criticising the automatic acceptance of the services' demands for land, and the following year it objected to the exemption of farm and forestry buildings from planning regulations. In 1959 it called for a regional plan to control burgeoning overspill from London, while in 1964 it advocated incentives to economic growth outside the south-east and in 1970 recommended the introduction of hedgerow preservation orders. The ensuing years saw CPRE attacking proposed increases in lorry weight limits, and advocating a decisive switch of investment from road to rail.

From this it is clear that CPRE has consistently been ahead of the times, repeatedly raising the very issues that are now most in the headlines.

It is thanks substantially to CPRE's early campaigning that, since 1947, the protection of the English countryside from development has been one of the greatest success stories of strategic planning – the envy of visitors from all over the world. The post-war Town and Country Planning Acts stopped ribbon development and unplanned urban sprawl at a stroke. They prevented virtually all isolated building in the country. You have only to travel through parts of Europe and North America to see what a transcending achievement this is. In Italy and Spain the centres of historic towns are superbly protected and cared for, but beyond the city walls spring up high-rise apartments. Every surrounding hillside is sprinkled at random with new villas. Every approach road is lined, often for several miles, with factories and showrooms. And the march across the landscape continues uncontrolled, with new villas built ever higher to obtain a better view and main roads left with hardly a green field beside them.

Yet the very success of planning control in Britain has left us unprepared for the stupendous building boom that is now upon us. For the countryside the outlook is devastating and threatens to overwhelm all the achievements of the last half-century. It is not simply a question of the sheer volume of applications to develop, a substantial number of which must be met, but that all forms of development are far more demanding on land than ever before.

To take industry first, whatever may be said of satanic mills and Victorian industrial cities, and the huge tracts of open country they devoured, they made surprisingly intensive use of land. Most textile mills and warehouses were four, five or six storeys high, and mills and factories were often tucked into narrow valley bottoms to take advantage of fast running water to power their steam engines. By contrast, in the modern industrial estate the basic unit is a single storey warehouse shed, with all the principal activities carried out on one level only.

The modern trend is towards ever larger and more expansive industrial estates – many now christened as business or science parks. More and more of the new buildings on these parks are offices – the headquarters for major firms and innovation centres with space for new businesses. Here is the beginning of yet another migration from the city centre, equivalent to the ribbon development of the 1920s, which will demand even larger acreages for car-parking and landscaping. Yet local authorities everywhere are seeking to attract this kind of development.

Out-of-town shopping is the second arm of this increasingly overpowering assault on the countryside. The layout of new shopping centres also requires the maximum possible amount of land. Shopping is principally on one level, huge areas of car-parking are required and, to soften the seas of tarmac and motor cars, further land is taken for grass and tree planting.

Once again the Victorians, with their city arcades and department stores, obtained far better value from their land. But at the moment all the pressures are for out-of-town enclosed shopping centres. This is partly because the green field site is always the easy development option (and the land may be cheap too), and partly because the motorway network, intended to provide a fast link between conurbations, is becoming a magnet in itself. Thus the historic county capital of Shrewsbury which has two new shopping centres in the heart of the town was recently faced with five applications for further shopping centres on green field sites around the town.

Where a city, such as say Preston or Southampton, is so large that the built-up area presses against the district boundaries, there is naturally a temptation to the councillors of neighbouring rural boroughs to agree to new shopping centres in nearby stretches of open country simply to cream off some of the spending and rateable value that the big town attracts.

In the past, the County Council, with the help of the

County Structure Plan, has been able to take an overview and hold the balance between rival districts. But the Government is determined to shift the major work of planning from the county to the district, for example by abolishing County Structure Plans. The decline of strategic planning is a potential disaster for many of the landscapes shown in this book. Many districts will naturally be tempted by the latest status symbol, whether it be a shopping, business or leisure development. Ironically, the diminution of the county role could have an equally adverse effect where districts are conservation-minded. The natural tendency of a district faced with a demand from central Government to agree to development it does not want will be to dump it on the edge of the area – whether up against another town or in open country. Thus in Hampshire the rural district of Test Valley, forced to find space for two thousand houses, proposes to place them right on the boundary, next to Eastleigh.

When the motorway network was inaugurated no one but CPRE envisaged the soft-touch it would become for planning permission. The whole concept of the new motorways was that they would be an utter contrast to the old trunk roads, which were rapidly lined with showrooms, depots, factories and garages disgorging a constant stream of traffic that endlessly delayed the motorist. The motorways were conceived as roads through a rural landscape – an entirely new experience in British motoring. But nearby towns and cities have quickly crept out towards them. The M4 has become the new southern boundary of Reading, originally two miles away across green fields. Indeed until recently Reading seemed set to spill over to the south: only a campaign by CPRE prevented this from happening.

There is a potentially crucial alliance to be forged here between city and country. Traditionally they have been seen as rivals and opposites, but both stand to suffer in roughly equal measure from present trends. Today, all the pressures point to a vast increase in suburbia. If they continue, and the indications are that they will accelerate

dramatically, it will leave many fine town centres in a state of decline. The best shops will go, the upper floors will be left empty and the rents will no longer pay for the repairs. When consumer durables as well as food shopping move out of town, a thousand-year-old tradition of the English market town will come to an end.

The pressure is not simply in the overcrowded south-east. Many northern towns and cities after half a century of severe industrial decline now see shopping as their one growth area. Whether in-town or out-of-town they will be fearful of putting serious obstacles in the way. Their reasoning is simple – a town which is too concerned about either its historic core or surrounding green fields, they say, will simply lose the development to a neighbour.

The renewed threat of the spread of suburbia – on a scale unseen since the 1920s and 1930s – comes most strongly with the demand for new housing. It is not the sheer volume required that is so damaging, for needs must be met – it is the type of housing and its location. Whether in Surrey or Lincolnshire, Norfolk or Worcestershire, CPRE branches are concerned that new housing is not for local people. What goes up is a four-bedroomed, two-bathroomed detached house intended for well-heeled commuters.

At one end of the scale are the recent proposals for new towns of five thousand houses or more, such as those made by Consortium Developments, an alliance of the nation's leading house builders. At the other end is the steady infilling and enlargement of almost every pretty and unspoilt village or hamlet that survives.

Virtually every branch of CPRE reports on the constant pressure on villages. In Dorset any entrancingly picturesque hamlet of ten thatched cottages that survived unspoilt until five years ago now has ten new houses rudely tacked on to it. In Lincolnshire the little village of Winderby is suddenly faced with an application to treble its size. In Gloucestershire numerous streets in Cotswolds villages now have a new pattern which reads eighteenth-century cottage – new bungalow – seventeenth-century cottage – new bungalow.

In resisting such trends CPRE is not simply trying to make the clock stand still. It is passionately concerned with the survival of country communities and the provision of the vital services they need. It is committed to fighting for housing for local people at affordable prices.

From the start CPRE's philosophy has been that new housing provision, like industrial and shopping development, must be based on careful forward planning, not on off-the-cuff decisions and special cases. The whole basis of practical conservation in both town and country has lain in the strategic overview developed at county level – now at risk from the Government's plans to diminish the status of county planning. The danger to the countryside is severe. It is an open question as to how much ordinary, undesignated countryside can survive the tide of semi-urban sprawl.

For the first half-century of CPRE's existence, farming was almost universally perceived as the natural ally of conservation. While the threat from development was clear and readily identifiable, awareness of the damage being done by ever more intensive farming methods dawned slowly.

Today the statistics of loss are well rehearsed. Between 1947 and 1985 some 95 per cent of lowland herb-rich meadows were destroyed. Eighty per cent of lowland grasslands and sheepwalks on chalk and limestone disappeared, largely by conversion to arable or 'improved' grassland; 30 to 50 per cent of ancient lowland woods, composed of native, broadleaf trees, were replaced by conifers or grubbed up to provide more farmland; some 50 per cent of lowland fens and valley and basin mire have disappeared or been significantly damaged by drainage and 'reclamation': and no less than 109,000 miles of hedgerow, enough to circle the globe four times, have gone. Perhaps most disturbing of all, the rate of hedgerow loss actually increased during 1980–85 from 2,600 miles a year to 4,000 – at the very moment when public concern was at its height.

Farming today has the capacity to change the countryside on a scale and at a speed unimaginable a few decades ago. A revolution in farm machinery has allowed cultivation further up slopes than had been thought possible, and deep into marshes previously considered unassailable.

During the last two decades CPRE has been at the centre of the agricultural debate. In 1977 it brought the problem of the ploughing of Exmoor's moorland to national notice, resulting in the decision to set up Lord Porchester's study – which resoundingly supported CPRE's campaign to prevent further damage. The next year it played a major role in resisting a Southern Water Authority drainage scheme for the hauntingly beautiful Amberley Wildbrooks in West Sussex. In the early 1980s it was intimately involved in lobbying for improvements to the Wildlife and Countryside Bill and its successors, so that it could protect precious landscapes from damage.

As the agricultural debate has become more heated, CPRE has remained constant in its view that farming must continue to occupy the bulk of the countryside. It is a stalwart advocate of less intensive farming methods, and disputes the notion that there is a surplus of agricultural land simply because there is a surplus of agricultural produce – the excess food is the result of a deliberate policy of guaranteeing farmers artificially high prices. What is needed, CPRE suggests, is a new system of direct farm support, which will ensure farming is viable without stimulating increased production. Simply because we can produce the same amount of food on a smaller and smaller area of land, it is not necessarily right to do so. Public opinion is reacting strongly against food products with ever-increasing quantities of additives, fertilisers and hormones. With this goes increasing concern about pollution of the soil and the water supply as well as the atmosphere, and a desire to protect and foster wildlife and England's well-loved landscapes.

The Government's 'set-aside' provisions, offering incentives to farmers to take land out of production, will, claims CPRE, simply encourage farmers to work the remaining farmland more intensively.

CPRE's recent report *Concrete Objections* suggests that

an alarming proportion of the land taken out of agricultural use will go for development. This is one of the most dangerous of all the challenges to our countryside inheritance. In the past the Ministry of Agriculture has always objected strongly to applications to develop good agricultural land. CPRE's report shows that since 1985 a quiet but potentially devastating change has been taking place. In 1987 there were applications for development on more than 25,000 hectares of farmland (outside agreed statutory development plans) – the largest area ever recorded. This represents a 100 per cent increase since the late 1970s. Yet the Ministry of Agriculture is objecting to an ever smaller proportion. In 1981 MAFF objected to 481 proposals; in 1987 it formally objected to 58 – less than one in twenty – failing to object to developments covering an area nearly equal to the total farmed countryside of the Isle of Wight. In 1987 for the first time since records began, MAFF agreed to more development on Grade 1 farmland (the best 3 per cent) than it opposed. The 1986 Agricultural Act gave the Ministry a duty to balance conservation interests with agricultural ones – yet since the act came into force development appears to have gained a higher priority than ever before.

What is more deeply objectionable is that the Government says one thing and does another. On 13 February 1987 the Environment Secretary, Nicholas Ridley, wrote to all members of the House of Commons stating, 'We recognise that the best and most versatile agricultural land (mainly Grades 1 and 2, but some other land as well) has a *special* importance because of its scarcity and because once built on it can seldom be returned to agricultural use. So we say such land should be protected for the longer term and retain that priority.'

The case for protecting this land is gravely weakened if MAFF does not object to development proposals. The Department of the Environment confirms that the greater proportion of the land lost to agriculture is not being transformed into nature reserves or assigned to reversible rural uses, but is being developed with houses, industry and roads.

One extraordinary aspect of the whole system of countryside protection is that there are so few provisions to safeguard individual features of the landscape. Serious questions need to be asked as to the validity of a system which allows ancient pasture or moorland to be ploughed, contours to be altered and field boundaries to be removed or changed so that the entire character of the land that is protected can be obliterated. In view of the constant public outcry, locally and nationally, over the removal of hedgerows, it is extraordinary that there are so few ways of protecting an individual hedgerow.

A simple solution is at hand in the system of landscape conservation orders (LCOs) cogently argued for by CPRE and the Council for National Parks in a paper submitted to the Department of the Environment in 1985.

LCOs would be analogous to tree preservation orders. They could be used to protect landscape in the way that designation of conservation areas is used in towns, to cover stretches of moorland, heathland, downs and meadows; or they could be brought in to protect individual features such as stone walls, ponds and dewponds, green lanes, ancient tracks and field markings. The Government, however, has yet to be converted and the tragic losses continue.

A further major threat to the countryside comes from unsympathetic farm buildings. Today most recently-built barns are simply large industrial sheds. The sole aim is to enclose the biggest possible space at the cheapest possible price. All too often new barns are sited with what seems a deliberate, even malevolent, crassness – as if the farmer was trumpeting his freedom from planning controls. Precisely because new agricultural buildings have been so handsomely grant-aided, there has been a tendency to build bigger than strictly necessary. Indeed too many barns are not used for purposes essential to the farm on which they stand but help to house a part of the ever-growing EEC mountains of grain, butter and every type of agricultural produce.

At the very least farmers should be obliged to give notice of proposed barns, so local planning authorities have the opportunity to discuss the choice of site. Where this has happened, for example in National Parks, local planning officers have been able to suggest a barn should be on lower ground, or grouped with other farm buildings, or that it should be clad in timber rather than corrugated sheeting. Farmers tend to choose open sites, or sites near main roads, as a first preference, but more careful siting rarely brings significant disadvantages.

Forestry, too, has the power to transform the landscape, with remarkably little opportunity for public comment or control. Tree planting has been a concern of CPRE's since its foundation in 1926, when it argued fiercely against the uncontrolled afforestation in the Lake District in the 1920s and 1930s.

More recently, a bitter battle over the proposed afforestation of Ashtead Fell, in a wholly unprotected corridor between the Lake District and the Yorkshire Dales National Parks, was the trigger in 1986 for fresh campaigning to eliminate destructive conifer afforestation.

The questionable foundations of British forestry policy were revealed the next year in a major CPRE report *Growing Against the Grain* by Philip Stewart, an Oxford University forestry economist. His firm conclusion was that most forestry in Britain was unlikely to be profitable to the nation on strict financial terms. This coincided with the National Audit Office's review of the Forestry Commission that 'it was not clear whether the costs [of forestry] to the Exchequer from the present grant and tax incentives regime were matched by commensurate benefits in national economic terms.'

As opposition to environmentally damaging, subsidised forestry mounted, fired further by the controversy over the Scottish Flow country at Caithness and Sutherland, CPRE commissioned a second report from the leading economic consultants, Pieda, *Budgeting for British Forestry* (1988). This proved to be CPRE's most successful piece of lobbying yet. It showed how the Government could, by simple taxation adjustment, stop indiscriminate encouragement of conifer forestry. Shortly afterwards, tax reliefs for forestry were indeed abolished and replaced by grants, and a new policy virtually ruled out new conifer planting in the uplands of England. This was an historic victory for the conservation movement – but the fight now continues for a more environmentally sensitive scheme of grants for woodland management.

More than half the countryside now enjoys some form of protected status – as National Park, Green Belt, nature reserve, Area of Outstanding Natural Beauty (AONB), Site of Special Scientific Interest (SSSI), Environmentally Sensitive Area (ESA) or simple Area of Landscape Value. In all this CPRE has played a crucial role, especially in the creation of the National Parks and Green Belts. But designation, as CPRE knows only too well, is only the beginning. Some of CPRE's greatest battles have been over National Parks. Elsewhere in the world, these are in public ownership, preserved for ever in the public interest. In Britain such a system, which would involve large-scale compulsory purchase, has never been considered practical. Thanks to constant pressure, the Government now implements planning controls in National Parks beyond those in other parts of the country. But, as John Gibb shows in this book, even National Parks remain open to exactly the development pressures which their status should protect them against – road building, quarrying, holiday chalet construction.

Indeed, whatever the special status, effective protection relies on public vigilance. Time and again, supposedly protected areas have only been saved from crass disfigurement by furious campaigns by CPRE and other conservationists. Nowhere is this better illustrated than in the New Forest, which despite its special protection was only saved from an intrusive bypass proposal by a massive CPRE-led campaign.

This defeat of the proposed Lyndhurst bypass is described fully in the Hampshire chapter. What matters in the national context is the blow this represented to the use of private members' bills as a means of forcing contentious issues through Parliament and thus avoiding the public inquiry system.

Nicholas Ridley, with the Government's Channel Tunnel Bill, had set a precedent the previous year that numerous developers and public authorities would dearly love to follow.

Some time before the bill began its passage in 1986 there had been angry noises from MPs and Ministers that the public inquiry system was getting out of hand – 'The Victorians would never have got the railways built if they had this public inquiry nonsense' was a much-quoted line. 'We need the development and we need the jobs,' the argument continued, 'so let's go back to the old system of the private Act of Parliament that served them so well.'

In saying this, they forgot their own history. The public inquiry system evolved precisely because MPs felt they could not cope with the ever more complex issues raised by the railway bills. In the mid-nineteenth century interested parties were often limited to two – the railway company and the country landowner who had a seat in one or other House of Parliament and thus direct access to the system to defend his property.

Today there are far more interested parties and individuals worried about the impact of major infrastructure projects. This is not just a symptom of the growth of the so-called protest industry, but the expansion of the legitimate concerns of local people and businesses and a general heightening of awareness and concern. But at the time of the Channel Tunnel Bill ministers were being told that public inquiries had become a national pastime, especially of the unemployed and the retired middle classes, and that jobs were being lost as a result.

'Stansted and Archway are burned on my heart,' said Mr Ridley, echoing Queen Mary's sentiments on losing Calais. So it was not surprising that after the passing of the Channel Tunnel Bill private bills were seen as the new fast track for contentious development proposals.

The all-party committee which examined the Lyndhurst Bypass Bill concluded that it was unnecessary to bring a bill to Parliament to authorise a road as a matter of procedure and that to do so would set a further dangerous precedent. It threw the Bill out. Lyndhurst represented a stunning double victory – the case was made to protect one of the most beautiful stretches of countryside in Britain, and a threat to the whole system of public participation in planning was averted. This is a reminder that we only have beautiful countryside and public participation because they have been fought for – not once, but again and again.

Some of CPRE's most daunting confrontations over the years have been with the public utilities, over the siting of new power stations, electric power lines, reservoirs, and the management of the water authorities' huge land holdings. Now the upheaval in the structure and ownership of the electricity and water industries brings both opportunities and fresh potential dangers to our landscape.

CPRE and allied organisations have battled for tough environmental duties for the new independent electricity industry and strong incentives to encourage energy conservation and promote small-scale, sensitive methods of generating electricity. This will determine how many more gigantic power stations will be built in remote countryside.

Further problems loom for the massive amount of scenic land which has passed into the hands of the newly privatised water companies. The ten former regional water authorities in England and Wales owned nearly 500,000 acres. North-west Water has 38,900 acres in the Lake District and 10,000 acres in the Forest of Bowland. 1987 figures showed that it also owned eighty-five farms with 58,474 acres of agricultural land. With privatisation and the pressure to increase profits, there is understandable concern that land may be sold off for development and attention to good conservation and public access may be reduced. At present the public can roam freely across substantial tracts of moorland over which there is no formal right of way. Such areas could be leased at very high rents for grouse-shooting. Until now the authority has successfully catered for all uses – walking, shooting, fishing and water-sports.

Thanks to CPRE lobbying, the Water Bill was much amended during its passage through Parliament and now provides better – if not watertight – safeguards for land in designated areas. Many water authorities bought land to protect it from development which could have put the purity of the water supply at risk, and much of the land they owned is wonderfully unspoilt as a result. Privatisation could force the new authorities to carry out the very development their predecessors have prevented over the last century.

Much pressure for this would come in the form of proposals for leisure development – holiday chalets, time-share apartments and hotels – and this leads to one of the most difficult issues CPRE faces. CPRE has long been a champion of access and public enjoyment of the countryside, but acute problems now arise not simply out of the sheer numbers involved but also because of the very different types of outdoor recreation that people seek. In America two distinct groups of visitors to National Parks have emerged: those who arrive on foot or bicycle with sleeping bags on their backs, and those who come in four-wheel-drive vehicles with speed boats, water-skis and ghetto-blasters. Provision must be made for both, without one ruining the enjoyment of the other.

Legacy invites us to think hard about the past and the future. Our countryside inheritance is not to be taken for granted. It will not survive today's massive pressures unless the present generation summons up a fierce determination for the sake of our children and their children.

To help meet this challenge, CPRE has to take up and tackle the whole range of industries and activities that pose a threat to the countryside, almost all of which have huge resources available in making their case. CPRE must talk and argue convincingly not just with farming and forestry interests, but with the house building, coal mining, gravel extraction, electricity and oil industries. It must deal at national level with a series of major Government departments – Agriculture, Energy, Environment and Transport – keeping up direct contacts with officials, seeking meetings with ministers, and checking and challenging the mountain of paperwork which all these Government departments produce. While personal contacts are important, CPRE does not soften its voice for fear of offending those in high places.

Some of CPRE's most signal successes in recent years have been at Westminster. Amidst all the lobbying groups competing for MPs' time and attention, it has established itself as a sound and reliable source of new policy initiatives, capable of marshalling evidence and mastering the detail of Parliamentary legislation. It has prompted, even drafted, numerous private members' bills; it constantly helps shape and sharpen key Government clauses at committee stage; it has given evidence to numerous Parliamentary committees of inquiry.

Past achievements help to provide the confidence and perseverance needed to fight new battles. Every one of CPRE's 44,000 members adds weight to its campaigns at local, regional and national level – and now that membership is sharply on the rise CPRE's influence will grow and grow.

The Legacy project itself brings a new dimension, celebrating the beauty of the land through new eyes. Look beyond the famous viewpoints, the picture postcard calendars and identify the power and the glory of the English landscape in all its moods. In John Gibb, CPRE has found an author with a brilliant facility for evoking the scenic qualities of the countryside, weaving a dramatic narrative out of complex planning battles. *Legacy* is an invitation to seek out visual poetry in the landscape, stimulated by the vision of some of the world's leading photographers.

The Derwent Valley

DERRY BRABBS specialises in landscape photography and is recognised as one of the finest exponents of the art in Britain. His moody, graphic images were commissioned for *Rural England*, the definitive work on the English countryside written for CPRE by Derek Mercer, and his pictures have illustrated bestselling books by Herriot and Wainwright. Brabbs's intimate knowledge of the English countryside and strong belief in the need to protect it were ideal qualifications for his work in Durham, where there is constant pressure to open up the land to get at the coal underneath.

IN 1942, IN RESPONSE to an emergency demand for more coal to fuel the war effort, open-cast mining came to County Durham, and it has blighted this beautiful and peaceful region ever since. Since the war, the practice has spread throughout the area and now threatens important areas of the north of England from Durham and Northumberland across the Pennines and into Cumbria.

Open-cast mining techniques have come on apace since the war. Today, these mines are sometimes wide and deep – scars on the land which can be up to a mile across and 200 yards deep. The method has already left wounds on the Durham countryside, and on Lancashire and Yorkshire, and there is constant and intensive pressure to exploit the Durham resources still further. If you have not seen them, it is hard to appreciate the impact of such giant gaping holes. Because they are exposed to the wind and weather, their detritus is spread over vast areas and compounded with noise and filth from the transport used to remove the coal and waste. There is little that can be done to disguise or reduce the offensive impact of open-cast mining.

The extraction of coal by this means also has a hidden and long-term effect on the landscape. Unlike when minerals such as building sand or hoggin are quarried, when coal is removed, permanent damage is caused which makes it impossible to return the land to its former fertility and appearance. Once an open-cast mine has been exhausted, the underlying rocks have been crushed in the extraction process, altering for good the amount of water which drains through them. The topsoil, cut and stacked, can lie around in mounds for many years while the mining is carried out. Neglected and unused, it is deprived of essential aeration and nutrients and becomes compacted. Even if it is heavily fertilised after replacement, the soil remains poor and incapable of supporting a full range of plant life. The sterility of the soil is compounded by the effect of nitrates from fertilisers which drain quickly through the crushed bedrock, leaching out minerals and entering the water supply.

For many years, open-cast mining proposals have been

Tanfield, a coal-mining village on the south side of the Derwent Valley. The church is ancient, but much of the village grew up with the mine, and remains now that the mine has gone.

Sacriston, north of Durham

The Derwent Valley

Tanfield village

Front Street, Sacriston

Langley Park, a large coal-mining village developed in the nineteenth century. Laid out in grid pattern, the houses often have the main garden at the road frontage and their entrance leads from a back passageway.

Opposite Reclaimed land at Byermoor, close to a site of 1 square mile of rolling countryside currently proposed for open-cast working at Marley Hill

Langley Park, 1935

the curse of the Derwent Valley which runs from Durham into Northumberland. The Derwent rises high on the moors at Allenheads, to the east of Penrith in Durham, and runs eastwards to Newcastle through wooded hills, resting now and again in reservoirs and lakes before passing on through ravines and green slopes. The great houses of Gibside and Hamsterley Hall are close by the Derwent and are memorials to the coal and steel industrialists who once exploited the lower reaches of the river but, at the same time, took good care to protect it – it was the setting for their homes.

Gibside, built in the 1750s, has one of the greatest landscape gardens of the north of England. It was the creation of George Bowes, a wealthy Durham coal magnate. When the indefatigable eighteenth-century traveller Lady Mary Wortley visited the house she said, 'I love woods but I do not desire such forest that you would expect to be entertained in the evening by the howling of wolves and yelling of tigers.' The National Trust has joined with local councils, amenity groups, the Forestry Commission and the Landmark Trust to preserve the ornamental pleasure grounds, including the chapel and banqueting house, and Gibside could become a symbol for the rare beauty of the Durham landscape.

Rich in timber, the Derwent Valley was for generations the heart of a magnificent forest which, although regularly plundered by shipbuilders and charcoal burners, because of its value and beauty was properly managed and regenerated after use. The old railway which skirted the valley and occasionally crossed it, notably on the magnificent Hamsterley Viaduct, is now a spectacular right of way and a protected walkway through the valley and up to Newcastle.

The valley of the Derwent is cursed by the riches which lie just beneath its lovely surface. There are massive reserves of prime quality coal throughout and for many years the National Coal Board Opencast Executive has been attempting to gain permission to exploit it. In 1971, Derek Ezra, Chairman of the NCB at the time, said, 'We either satisfy the environmental requirements or we satisfy the coal requirements, but we are not capable of doing both at the same time.' He was absolutely correct and the problem is clear – open-cast mining is an environmental disaster.

Until the 1970s, few protesters had seriously contemplated the daunting prospect of confronting the NCB, but, as in many other beautiful corners of England, residents of the Derwent Valley felt passionately about their countryside and were prepared to fight to protect it. In the years since 1971, when CPRE vowed to fight open-cast mining all the way, the area has become a battleground between the coal industry and the local people. The prize for the coal industry would be short term. Its effect on the valley would be for ever.

In 1986, six applications were made to operate open-cast pits in Durham. Most sites were grouped in such a way that, had the applications been approved, there would have been continuous workings over wide stretches of countryside. In 1988 a further five proposals for open-cast sites were submitted and the hardline style with which they were promoted resulted in further polarising opinions and alienating the local people from the private operators and British Coal.

CPRE is, understandably, extremely active in this part of England and has, over the years, achieved some notable victories. The Durham branch fought its first application in the early 1970s and has since, with experience, developed and refined its expertise during a long and seemingly never-ending struggle against the coal industry. Its approach has been to attack the applications on economic and legal as well as environmental grounds. It has proved its case in over a dozen public inquiries but has also occasionally been defeated, most notably at Daisy Hill, north of Durham. In a remarkable, but all too familiar, turnaround, the Secretary of State for the Environment ignored the recommendations of his independent inspector and granted planning permission for an open-cast mine.

This decision is a clear sign of the close relationship between the Government and the Opencast Executive,

Windyside, Westgate, Weardale – Swaledale sheep were the mainstay of farming in this area during the first half of the twentieth century

Sunset from the B6310 at Burnopfield

View west across the Derwent Valley from Bowsens Hole

West Black Dene, Wearhead

Allensford, a former lead-mining village near Consett

and is a chilling reminder of the difficulties which will be faced by local environmental groups in the years to come. Nevertheless a small number of expert individuals working together, supported with advice and help from amenity societies and planners, has been able to counteract the big guns of a massive and powerful industry.

In recent years, the Government has published guidelines for local authorities on how to approach proposals for open-cast mining applications. In spite of the established fact, underlined by the House of Commons Energy Committee, that it is one of the most environmentally destructive processes being carried on in the UK, the Department of Energy has continued to support the principle of open-cast extraction. 'There is a need for it,' they say, but have so far failed to outline the grounds on which this need is based. They have also failed to recommend that British Coal should pay any regard to communities' loss of amenity. In their frequent responses to Government policy guidelines on open-cast mining, C P R E has called for a definition and justification of 'need' and for official recognition of the environmental impact of this type of mining.

The first-time visitor to the Derwent Valley will be impressed by a sense of singular tranquillity. It was close to these wooded hills that Bede and Cuthbert were buried, in the great mediaeval city of Durham. The city is still encircled by some of the most stunning yet uncelebrated scenery in the land.

The conflict between those who love this rare corner of England and the organisations which are committed to exploiting it will continue until there is a clear political decision against a process which can lacerate great swaths of the countryside for all time.

Castleside – the steel works of Consett dominate the skyline

Proposed site for open-cast mining at Hollings, east of Whittonstall

The River Derwent at
Lintzford

The Lake District National Park

TONY MCGEE earns his living as one of Britain's finest fashion photographers and film makers. This assignment was the first time he had visited the Lake District. He said afterwards that the quality of the early spring light induced a sort of photographic gluttony, forcing him to pursue the irresistible blend of rock and water until he captured it.

THE LAKE DISTRICT NATIONAL PARK lies in Cumbria between the Irish Sea and the Pennines. You can see the blue hills in the distance as you drive up into the top left-hand corner of England along the M6. There are three prosperous and growing towns of moderate size – Kendal, Windermere and Ambleside – and the permanent population of the Park is 41,000. It is an ancient landscape and the exposed rocks are 4–500 million years old. Glaciation has steepened slopes and dammed and deepened valleys, producing high tarns and large lakes which radiate from the central volcanic dome. It is a breathtakingly beautiful landscape.

The mountains are separated into three main groups and are centred around the peaks of Scafell, Skiddaw and Helvellyn. These are the highest and most rugged in England, wonderful for walking and climbing. There are a number of high scree slopes, notably in Wasdale. The lower slopes carry woodlands of scrub oak and Scots pine, and in the western part of the Park there are extensive plantations of conifers and some good pasture, where fields have traditionally been enclosed with dry stone walls. The lakes are numerous but, with the exception of Windermere and Ullswater, relatively small. Several are used for water abstraction. The Park has a 10-mile coastline between Ravenglass and Silecroft which primarily consists of sand-dunes.

In 1940, Norman Birkett, President of the Friends of the Lake District and former Chairman of the Standing Committee on National Parks, later to become Lord Justice Birkett, wrote a message to members in his annual report: 'The supreme issues which are being decided in the war demand all that can be given in time and work and devotion. Every member may rest assured that everything has been done to fulfil the responsible work which the Friends of the Lake District regard as their special care. Because of the difficulty of the task in these times, I ask for a continuance of the confidence and support of the members until happier days come.'

During the war the Lake District was used as a refuge for children and civilians escaping from the heavy bombing

Wastwater and Great Gable, 1930s – a proposal by British Nuclear Fuels to abstract water from Wastwater and Ennerdale was defeated in 1981

Sty Head Pass from Great Gable

Within the National Park

Haymaking, Skelwith, near Ambleside, 1942

raids. It also became a safe haven for industries involved in the war effort and was subjected to increased mineral extraction; the fells were used for the training of troops. Birkett was deeply concerned about the damage being inflicted on the area but, because of censorship, was unable to communicate any details to his members. 'The Lake District has not lost its appeal,' he said; 'indeed war, deadening so many of our impulses, has sharpened the edge of man's affection for it.' It is not surprising therefore that membership stayed steady throughout at a remarkable two thousand and that in a 1940 appeal during a campaign to protect the Duddon Valley the target figure was greatly exceeded. The Friends found much to occupy them during the war and stayed active throughout in spite of the restrictions on printing and leafleting. Birkett, who went on to feature prominently as a prosecutor at the Nuremberg trials, was an active and formidable proponent of National Parks until he died in 1962.

The Lake District's extraordinary mixture of high fells, valleys and water form a beautiful landscape of apparent pastoral simplicity. A hundred years ago the Victorians saw in the untouched splendour of the landscape a romantic ideal and this was to generate much fine art and a frenzy of literary passion.

The attributes of the Lake District are not simply scenery and an idyllic way of life, however. The lakes are also reservoirs, conveniently sited for the industrial northwest of Manchester and Liverpool. Bitter battles were fought over the deepening and damming of some, such as Haweswater, resulting in the introduction of access and conservation safeguards – battles which have had to be fought again with the plans for water privatisation. Rich mineral deposits of limestone, coal, graphite and slate lie beneath the fells and, during the nineteenth century, iron ore, copper and lead were mined in large quantities. Quarrying remains a buoyant primary industry as demand for slate fireplaces and roofs revives.

Farming has had a significant influence on the landscape of the Lake District and over 30,000 acres are used for grazing. The walls, hedges and woodlands of the

Cattle on the mountain road beneath Yewbarrow, with Great Gable in the distance, 1930

The splendour of the Lake District has made it a target for commercial exploitation

Harrowing grassland, High Park Farm, Little Langdale

traditional upland farms have kept the bracken, gorse and rushes at bay and have added a unique visual character to the land.

In the years since the war, the cost-conscious practices of modern agriculture, in even this harsh landscape, have changed the appearance of these farms. Stone walls and buildings have been replaced with barbed wire and steel sheds. Bracken has begun to intrude on to the hills, mires have been drained and the dead hand of afforestation is evident on the bleak shores of the lakes. Although the scope for agricultural improvement is limited, over-grazing has become a serious problem. Few of the Park Authority's powers and initiatives can counteract the overwhelming pressure to intensify grazing on hill areas.

It is a strange characteristic of human behaviour that, having managed to save one of the loveliest corners of the British Isles from the unwelcome attention of industry and development, we should still try to damage it. Today, the annual news letters published by the Friends of the Lake District, CPRE's representative body in Cumbria, continue to show a long list of appalling proposals. Threats range from afforestation to holiday camps and theme parks, and no matter how many times unsympathetic proposals are rejected by the Park Authority others immediately take their place.

The theory behind this assault seems to be that if you keep trying you will eventually get a foot in the door and that this applies as much to the Lake District as elsewhere. In 1987, for instance, permission was given to plant trees on 300 acres of Ashtead Fell on the borders of the National Park. This not only ruined the landscape it created a precedent which could have had repercussions for a vast sweep of undulating fells stretching from the Lake District to the Yorkshire Dales and beyond. Only a ministerial edict – warmly welcomed by CPRE – that conifer planting will not normally be permitted in the English uplands prevents wholesale damage.

Before the Lake District was designated a National Park on 9 May 1951, it had been the threat of reservoirs, pylons

Brigsteer, a Westmorland village, 1942

Increasing pressure from the tourist and leisure industries
threatens this tranquillity

and massive pine plantations which had most worried those who loved the area. The men and women who pressed for the creation of National Parks decreed that they should be laid aside for conservation and public enjoyment. And while the Parks were never given the powers and resources to fulfil the first of these responsibilities, there is no question but that the second has happened. The revolution in transport, mobility and interest in the countryside has brought visitors to the Lake District in ever-increasing numbers.

In 1988 there were over twenty million visitors. This, together with the accelerating development pressures on the area, has prompted new concern for the future. The failure of the Lake District to win World Heritage designation has confirmed the need for new and stricter powers to protect our most precious landscapes.

The most popular parts of the Lake District, particularly around Windermere, have become targets for developers of time-share chalets and 'holiday villages'. To the astonishment of many, building proposals have been put forward seriously in spite of their obvious incompatibility with the objectives of the National Parks.

The escalation of water traffic has become a problem on the lakes: over thirty thousand motor-powered boats are registered on Lake Windermere alone and the number of sailing dinghies, rowing boats and windsurfers is rising significantly. There is no system to control the over-use of the rivers and lakes, and while low-flying aircraft and private helicopters shatter the peace, the Park Authority has no influence over the air routes. The number of visitors has now reached a level which threatens to destroy the Park's special atmosphere.

Yet although tourism in the Lake District is said to be worth £300 million a year, there is simply not enough money in the Park Authority's coffers to maintain the standards which National Parks were originally set up to oversee. Neither do the Countryside Commission, the National Trust (which owns a quarter of the High Fells) and the Nature Conservancy Council have deep enough pockets to meet the need.

Perhaps even more worrying, as a result of generations of underinvestment and a declining agricultural workforce, the very fabric of the fells has begun to crumble. Miles of rights of way are waiting to be repaired, signposting needs to be improved, farmers and landowners need money to maintain their property, and farm buildings are falling into decay. With more visitors, wildlife sites and common land are being degraded.

In many respects the area has reached crisis point. In an exciting and innovative gesture, the Lake District Special Planning Board has called for new powers and an increased budget to address the problems of the future. Although this is a landscape which is without equal anywhere in the world, without increased support this much-loved corner of England faces degradation and decline.

Haymaking, Flodden Hall Farm, Lyth, Westmorland

Opposite, top Ruskin's View at Kirkby Lonsdale, Westmorland, across the valley of the River Lune; *bottom* Crosthwaite, near Windermere, 1945

Without increased support, the Lake District faces degradation and decline

Berkshire

HARRY DE ZITTER photographed Berkshire with a fresh eye uninfluenced by ever having seen the county before. 'I spent most of my time in the west of the county where I was interested in the almost compulsive neatness of the landscape. Farmers, having uprooted most of the hedgerows and drained the corners of their fields, trim what is left with machines and leave bits of geometrically designed woodland as cover for the gamebirds. There are corners where the atmosphere of prehistory still exists – under the Downs at Inkpen, for instance – but the wealth which has moved into this part of the county seems to have been intent on destroying the rural nature of the place. There is no untidiness any more.'

Based in London, Harry de Zitter is a commercial photographer with an international reputation for his portraits and editorial reportage.

MANY BLOODY BATTLES have been fought over the rural treasures of Berkshire and the county has always featured prominently in English history. Alfred the Great, King of Wessex, born in the Vale of the White Horse, crushed the Danish invaders on the wide sweep of the western Downs. The fertile, beautiful kingdom he ruled, with its soft hills and succulent river valleys, was a land of milk and honey, rich in natural resources and close to the political hub of the country. By the time of his death at the beginning of the tenth century, Wessex had been divided into shires and Berkshire assumed the mantle of its modern identity for the first time.

A century later, the victorious William, on his way to London from the south coast, founded castles at Wallingford and Windsor, and in the turbulent centuries which followed, conflict was never far away from the Berkshire towns and villages.

Reading, sitting strategically on the Thames within 50 miles of London, grew prosperously around its Abbey, developing into a market town which fed off the agricultural wealth of the surrounding country. Communications improved with the excavation by the Victorian engineers of canals between London, Bristol and Oxford. It was because of the network of waterways linking London with the west and Midlands that Reading first developed into a major commercial centre and its continued prosperity was guaranteed.

Newbury became famous for its wool, Henley for its malt and beer and Maidenhead for the timber which was shipped downstream to the London docks. Windsor, from where Defoe, during his perambulations around England, wrote that he could see St Pauls on a fine day, became the Royal country home, and today, by order of the Queen, Berkshire is known as 'The Royal County of Berkshire'. It was, and is, a land of contrasts, with the somnolent Thames Valley in the east and bracing western Downs.

At the turn of the century, the wide spread of the Kennet Valley seen from the top of Walbury Hill to the south of Newbury was one of the finest sights in England. It was the view which greeted the Welsh drovers towards

The Lambourn Valley in the 1930s

The Berkshire Downs, near Aldworth, when the corn market was depressed in the 1930s – the scrub-filled fields show fallen management standards. In recent decades, continuous cropping of barley has dominated the region's agriculture.

Conservationists blocked a massive development scheme at Grazeley, south of Reading

Opposite Intensive farming on thin soils near Bagnor in West Berkshire

Spencers Wood, a village now practically a suburb of Reading. Developers withdrew an application for major development of this area in the face of a national CPRE campaign.

the end of their long trek as they paused before driving their sheep down into the pretty village of East End on the way to the market at Newbury. To the west was Hungerford, where nothing much seemed to have happened since William of Orange came there to meet the King's commissioners at the Bear Hotel. To the east was Reading, just visible on a clear day. And in the heart of the valley the River Kennet, set about with marshland and water meadows, gathered pace with the help of the Lambourn and the Winterbourne, on its way to join the Thames. It was a peaceful and idyllic scene.

Today, the landscape remains impressive, but for different reasons. On the horizon, the huge cooling towers of Didcot Power Station belch thick clouds of condensation which drift in a long white veil across the Downs. In the foreground, the sad, swollen town of Newbury, with its shopping mall, fast-food stores and hideous 1950s post office building, has abandoned its charm to the developers. To the east, the Greenham Common air base sits like a scab on the old Down with its redundant missile bunkers and long concrete runway. And in the distance is Reading, fuming with new commercial life and reproducing itself every twenty years.

Today, perhaps more than any county in modern Britain, Berkshire carries the scars of political opportunism and inept planning. Although a human desire for an improvement in the quality of life is a major contributory factor, the roots of the county's headlong and disorderly progress can be traced back to a lack of political will during the 1960s.

The needs of modern industry for good international and local communications were answered only to the west of London where there was Heathrow airport and a network of trunk roads to north, south, east and west.

Then in 1970 the M4 began to make its way across the county to Bristol, Wales and the west. The motorway was a metalled wand which almost overnight opened up the magic of the Berkshire countryside. West Berkshire was no more than an hour from London and people soon came and saw and, liking what they saw, decided to stay. Land was cheap and communications were good. Newbury became a focus of interest for commerce and new technology. Sitting on the crossroads between Oxford and Southampton, London and Bristol, and only fifty minutes from Heathrow, it was a fine place in which to settle down and go to work.

Reading began to expand towards the M4. No longer a sleepy market town enriched by the Quaker biscuit makers and the railways, it took on the aspect of a city, spreading its voracious way cross-country towards the satellite towns of Wokingham and Bracknell. Gradually factories and estates began to appear along the motorway and the planners began to accept the road as a handy new southern boundary to Reading. The vast, steaming Courage brewery appeared almost overnight, dumped in the fields like the inside of an old television set.

All of a sudden, the heart of the Royal County had become a suburb. Communications technology, service industries and giant pharmaceutical corporations flocked to its green fields, clamouring for staff and the highest possible standard of living.

It was all too much for the local planners, vulnerable to the expert blandishments of developers and politicians determined to put industrial regeneration and market forces before all else. Factories and housing estates sprang up, unemployment plummeted and the once sleepy old county woke up in the 1980s to find itself in the midst of a social and economic upheaval. The oiled Barbour and green Hunter boot had replaced the smock and the clog and it was the estate agents who became the honoured guests at the country house shoots.

Berkshire has been divided into three distinct parts, each subject to differing planning controls. In the east, where the county begins inauspiciously at the village of Wraysbury, besieged by motorways and gravel pits, and progresses through Slough to Cookham and Maidenhead, it is protected by the London Green Belt. To the west, with the sad exceptions of Newbury and the villages of the Kennet Valley, it has been designated an Area of Outstanding Natural Beauty. In the centre, unprotected,

Mortimer, on the borders of Berkshire and Hampshire, 7 miles south of Reading, was growing as a residential area by the turn of the century

Boxford, West Berkshire

Near Hungerford

The River Lambourn in the 1930s

vulnerable, unfettered by controls, it has been mercilessly plundered and has turned into a sprawling conurbation straining to the limit of its girth.

In 1988 a county structure plan was devised, but it was amended by the Department of the Environment before publication, overriding the wishes of the county planners and cramming an extra seven thousand houses into Berkshire, thus allocating 43,000 new houses to the county by 1996. It paid little attention to the roads, schools, hospitals and other vital infrastructure which would be needed for the increase in development and it contemptuously ignored the wishes of local people.

During the long months while the entrails of the county were being picked over by the Secretary of State in his office high in the North Tower at Marsham Street, once quiet little communities in central Berkshire started to protest. In solidly Conservative Wargrave, normally law-abiding middle-class ratepayers and residents blocked the roads and marched in an attempt to save a small strip of land which separated them from the housing estates of Bracknell.

CPRE vigorously fought the draft revisions made by the Secretary of State, interpreting the close involvement of the Department of the Environment as a sign of the demise of local government influence in local planning matters. A campaign was waged against this interference with public meetings and the active participation of many of Berkshire's most prominent residents. In the end the Secretary of State was dissuaded from allowing further development over the M4 barrier south of Reading. But nothing could be done to stop the extra houses being forced into the plan. When it was all decided, Berkshire sat back and looked at its bleak future with dismay.

The old cloth town of Newbury is an example of how a pleasant market town and its hinterland can be transformed almost beyond recognition in a matter of a few years. Newbury has now acquired many of the characteristics of Reading. The speed of growth and the sudden appearance of massive housing estates – as many dwellings as possible jammed into a given area of green fields –

The Lock House, Greenham.

The Canal, Thatcham, (2)

The Kennet and Avon Canal on course through Berkshire: at Greenham, south of Newbury, and farther east at Thatcham. The canal connected Bristol and Bath with the Thames and London, contributing to the growth of Reading and other towns in the area.

Near East End, south of Newbury

Englefield, one of the largest estates in the Kennet Valley

is depressing. Schools have swollen to bursting point, crime has mushroomed and the National Health Service cannot cope. The maternity unit at the hospital has been forced to close while plans to build even more estates to the east and north of the town are debated. The revised structure plan allocated 9,500 new houses to be built here before 1996. Now Newbury has merged with the village of Thatcham and estates and factories line the River Kennet where not so long ago the song of the birds filled the valley.

A bypass is to be built around the town. During a long and exhaustive public inquiry the Department of Transport forcibly made its case for the A34 to be diverted through some of the most beautiful country in Berkshire. It will go in a sweep to the west, close to ancient woodland at The Chase, through the beautiful Enborne Valley, across the River Kennet, through the Rack Marsh nature reserve, up on stilts behind the noble ruin of the castle at Donnington, through the edge of the nature reserve at Penwood and then back to join the old road. As with the M4 at Reading, the bypass will act as a barrier and Newbury will be allowed to expand to the west. The hamlet of Bagnor with its elegant Watermill Theatre will be destroyed by the road and an idyllic corner of the Lambourn Valley will be wiped from the face of the earth for ever.

The tragedy of what has happened to Berkshire is not the increase in population but the quality of the development which has been allowed and the speed with which it has been pushed through. Nevertheless Berkshire still retains many treasures. The swell and roll of the Downs and the wooded folds of the hidden river valleys can still be enjoyed. To sit beside the Lambourn on a spring morning and listen to the murmur of soft breezes in the reeds is still one of the great pleasures available to all who live there. The majestic oak woods and the old thatched villages can still be explored in the west of the county. The arrival of a new population to Berkshire, not all of whom are eager to spend their leisure time in housing estates and shopping malls, has made what remains unspoilt in the Berkshire countryside even more precious and worth protecting.

The South Berkshire Hunt, 1930s

Grazeley, south of Reading

Environmental campaigner Sir Michael Hordern standing beside the River Lambourn at Bagnor, site of the crossing of the proposed Newbury bypass

The Thames Valley

NORMAN PARKINSON was brought up in the Thames Valley. He was educated at Westminster School and rowed at Henley where he grew to love the lush beauty of the countryside around Marlow and Hambleden. He started photographing for *Vogue* in the 1930s and soon became known for his original approach to fashion photography. 'I liberated the models,' he says. 'I took them away from the studio and put them in the countryside where they could get on with something active and look as if they were enjoying themselves.' In recent years he has taken on the mantle of court photographer and brought his elegant style to bear on formal portraits of the Royal family.

THE THAMES HAS BEEN THE CRADLE of our greatest political and cultural institutions and of all rivers has had most influence in the making of England. The tributaries of the Cherwell and the Kennet reach out to the industrial Midlands and to the Downs country of the rural south. To the east, the Thames estuary was for two thousand years the gateway to Europe and to the west it gave us a route to the watershed of the Severn and the Atlantic Ocean.

Our ancestors were able to navigate the Thames in their small craft, and spits of hard land on both banks allowed crossings to be made and settlements to be built and defended. During the Middle Ages, communities flourished along the valley as the Thames became navigable almost to its source. The river was the fastest, safest and most efficient route through the heart of England and towns appeared as staging points in the stream of traffic. Cotswold stone was shipped to London and used to build the great city churches. Cheese, beef, mutton and fowl were taken downriver from the rich valley farms, and foreign silks, wines and spices shipped upstream in return. Abbeys, schools and universities were founded and Royal palaces built at Greenwich, Hampton Court, Windsor, Woodstock and Beaumont Place. The Thames Valley settlements were fortified and highly populated. The towns became both economically and culturally important and developed into centres for religious foundations – Benedictine monasteries were started at Reading, Chertsey, Abingdon, Eynsham and Osney. Bridges were built at Oxford, Wallingford, Henley and Windsor, and by the time of Henry VIII the commercial success of the Thames Valley communities was guaranteed.

In the twentieth century the economic significance of the valley took on a different aspect: it became a desirable place to live. In his introduction to a CPRE survey of the Thames Valley published in 1930, the author John Buchan wrote, 'Motor roads and jerry builders are doing their best to ruin our country peace, but there are still little stone towns "forgotten in the western wolds", and scarcely altered since a Grevel or a Midwinter built the great church out of his wool profits.'

The River Thames at Streatley, from the Downs

The Thames near Abingdon, once the county town of Berkshire

The Thames Valley, looking towards the spreading town of Marlow, Buckinghamshire, from Winter Hill. The lakes have formed following gravel works in the flood plain of the river.

Oxford Rd, Reading. (1)

High St, Marlow. H299.

Today, the Thames Valley still passes through beautiful countryside and is as much an influence on our heritage as ever. But in common with so much of modern Britain, its beauty and character are threatened. The valley, as far as the river's source, is within easy reach of London and has now become home to millions of commuters.

In 1988 Norman Parkinson returned to photograph the countryside in the rich heart of the valley for CPRE. His links with the area are well established. In 1915, in order to avoid the zeppelins, his family took the infant Norman to live at Pishill near Henley. They lived at Bank Farm, a glorious corner of the valley which became home for most of his early childhood.

When he returned in the autumn of 1988, he was able for the first time to reappraise the countryside he had so loved. By the time the assignment was over, he had become almost sleeplessly apprehensive about the fate of his old playground. 'I came to look at the fields and woods and riverbank which I had explored as a child and I hated what I found.'

The Institute of Agricultural History at Reading University has over six thousand photographs of the Thames Valley recording landscapes, towns and villages from the source through Oxford and Reading to the Port of London. Most were taken by Collier in the early 1920s. It is a priceless collection which portrays a true picture of the Thames in that era. Although the images are of a classically romantic England, there are signs of agricultural decline and poverty as well as the beginnings of ribbon development. It is an honest record, which should inspire neither nostalgia nor complacency.

The photographs show Reading when it was still a quiet market town as well as the little backwaters of Bourne End and Cookham and the elegant settlements of Henley and Marlow. A photograph of Boulter's Lock taken in late June shows Maidenhead when it was the height of fashion and when Skindles Hotel was *the* place to have tea on sunny summer afternoons. Men in straw boaters and women in their best frocks with parasols and broad-brimmed hats throng the steps by the lock gates and watch the skiffs and punts on their way to the regatta at Henley.

There is a beautiful image of a brick-and-flint cottage on the river near Hambleden. Two girls are sculling energetically past. The picture reminded Parkinson of how the river used to look when he was a boy. 'There was a vital and cheerful air about the place,' he says. The cottage is now a house with large extensions at both ends. Heavy lorries thunder past the front door on the busy Henley to Marlow road.

The pace of change was brutally brought home to Norman Parkinson when he stood on the brow of Winter Hill by Cookham Dean and looked out across Cock Marsh at the great belching, thundering road which now bisects the Marlow Valley. Little attempt has ever been made to mask the A404 trunk road which intrudes into what was one of the most glorious views in the south of England. Old gravel workings littered with agricultural waste and builders' rubble offend the eye to the east of the road and to the west Marlow has sprawled out to meet the high embankment where industrial units obliterate the view.

In the 1930s, Marlow was one of the gems of the Thames Valley. Lying at the foot of the Chilterns and facing the superb Quarry Woods, it was secluded and comparatively traffic-free. It is an ancient town with a wide High Street and beautiful seventeenth- and eighteenth-century bow-fronted buildings. The authors of the 1930 CPRE survey called for the protection of this glorious spot, not from progress but from the devastation of ill-conceived development. They feared that building to the east of the town would ruin the charm of the river and the beautiful views of the woods.

Their apprehension was well founded. With the coming of the M4 and M40, Marlow became a much sought after dormitory town, close to London and with great commercial potential. It had no chance of retaining its old character. 'But why did they have to ruin the whole valley?' asked Parkinson. 'Marlow has been raped. No care has been taken to screen the factories or the road or design new buildings to complement the old style. The water-meadows have been laid waste and even the

Boulters Lock on the Thames at Maidenhead – the Sunday parade of boats during Ascot week remained a great occasion into the 1920s

Opposite, top Reading in the 1930s – late Victorian development along the Oxford Road near Reading West railway station; *bottom* Marlow in the 1920s

Undisturbed woodland track, Berkshire

A brick-and-flint bridge at Hambleden, Buckinghamshire

Opposite The Thames at Sonning

The Bridge.
Hambledon. A.617.

Sonning Bridge & White Hart 1518

sewage plant at Bourne End has never been screened. It is a tragedy.'

In contrast, further up the Thames, the little hamlet of Hambleden appears hardly to have changed. Privately owned by Viscount Hambleden, a vice president of the Thames Valley Branch of CPRE during the 1930s and for many years the owner of W. H. Smith, the village was firmly safeguarded against the developers. It has grown into an object of interest for strangers and passers-by. Today the problem here is how to allow the sensitive development of housing for local people without opening the floodgates.

Henley will always be close to Norman Parkinson's heart. 'In the early Thirties I rowed in several regattas for Westminster School,' he said. 'The Henley Regatta course is unique, not just because of its beauty but because of the sluggishness of the water. It always seemed to me that we were rowing through treacle. The stake boats were moored at the beginning of Temple Island, with its delicate and graceful folly, and the course runs through lush water-meadows against a backdrop of beechwoods down to the old town bridge and church tower.'

Sadly, even this mile and a half of the Thames, sacred to thousands of oarsmen throughout the world and surely the loveliest stretch of water imaginable, is now no longer safe. One hundred yards from where the stake boats are moored, a farmer has built a rubble and chalk road overlaid with gravel through the water-meadows at the head of the reach. He claims that it is needed to transport sheep. It is obvious that the road is likely to be used as access to a valuable area which can be rented out for business entertainment during the Regatta. Parkinson was outraged: 'It is beyond me that such vandalism can be allowed and that such a road can be built without permission.'

But it was the final days of his pilgrimage which caused him most anguish and made him feel that to protest would be to tilt at windmills. He had photographed the massive development at Lower Earley near Reading, where the houses, geometrically perfect and set close like wooden building bricks, tumble over a hill beside the M4. There are living units crammed into every corner of the landscape. Claustrophobic and depressingly lacking in character, they are typical of the barren nature of much modern development. Appropriately, it was the last photograph before driving to the peaceful and secluded hamlet of Great Haseley in a fold of farm land to the south of Oxford.

It is here that Consortium Developments, a group of nine major builders, applied for permission to build six thousand houses in a large new 'Country Town' which they were to call Stone Bassett. The developers claimed that the town would relieve the pressure for new houses in the city of Oxford, reduce demand for piecemeal expansion and provide a solution to the county's housing requirements until the end of the century. The land is outside the Chiltern Area of Outstanding Natural Beauty and beyond the Oxford Green Belt. It has, however, been labelled as being of Outstanding Landscape Value – a locally determined classification. The plan was contrary to the Oxford structure plan and was opposed by most Oxfordshire District and Parish Councils.

From the M40 the area appears to be flat and uninteresting, but drive down into the network of old sandstone hamlets and rolling hills with spinneys, small fields and hedgerows unfold. It is quiet and secluded, and typical of many Thames Valley villages which, over the centuries, have slowly grown and merged with the landscape. Close by there is a 20-acre stretch of ancient wetland called Spartum Fen. Graded as a Site of Special Scientific Interest, it has been left untouched for years and is rich in rare plant, bird and animal life.

Villagers came to talk as Parkinson set up his cameras and tripods. Patricia Kean has lived on the edge of Great Haseley for twenty-five years. Her cottage was once part of the village of Lachford, most of which was burned to the ground after the Black Death. It sits beside Spartum Fen. 'The fen will be ruined if they go ahead,' she said. 'There will be six thousand houses and the dogs and cats to go with them. The wildlife which thrives here now will disappear. They say that they can overcome the drainage

East Hagbourne, Berkshire

Opposite, top Hambleden Bridge, early 1900s; *bottom* The fashionable village of Sonning

A badly planned housing development pours over the horizon at Lower Earley in Berkshire

An Oxfordshire Lane, Binfield Heath. A.420

2090 Silchester Common.

problems but how can you protect woodland, hardly touched since the Ice Age, from the effect of all that building and waste?'

Great Haseley and Little Haseley 2 miles down the road became close-knit communities as the villagers fought the threat to their homes. CPRE, which is not against the principle of country towns, provided they are appropriately sited, fulfil a genuine need and are consistent with the local structure plan, vigorously attacked the application at the public inquiry. The developers' case, it claimed, was inept, badly presented and contrary to a mass of established planning policies. It was totally at variance with the new Oxfordshire structure plan, would attract London commuters rather than solve housing problems in Oxford, and was against Government policy on development close to motorway junctions. The environmental impact on the area would be appalling.

John Alexander, a parish councillor from Great Haseley, spoke of the anger of the local community: 'Consortium Developments knew that they would have to pay heavily to make their case, but they have deep pockets and they can set their costs against tax.' The villagers were not so fortunate. 'Local people were horrified by the threat and handed over heirlooms, wedding presents, even pocket money to help fight it.'

Parkinson stood on the tower of the old church and looked at the land which, if the developers ever win, will be packed tight with a carpet of cubes. 'It is tragic to see a community put under such stress and pressure,' he said. 'Even if the application is thrown out, the village will never be the same again. And other, similar communities will be asking themselves: What if the developers apply to build in the countryside near our village?'

In the event the consortium's appeal to the Secretary of State was thrown out, but it was replaced almost immediately by an application to build a motorway service station near by!

Today's River Thames is vulnerable to change along most of its length, and its meadows and valleys are eyed greedily by many who want to exploit them. In the

Gloucestershire countryside close to the village of Somer-ford Keynes, where the Thames starts its meandering way to London and beyond, a plan to build six hundred holiday villas and a seventy-suite hotel and leisure complex has cast a pall of despair over local residents. The proposed development would provide short-let holiday chalets for tourists keen to experience the incompatible attractions of watersports and birdwatching in an area known as the Cotswold Water Park. It is at present a network of small communities and lakes – a legacy of old gravel workings – linked by winding side roads and lanes which run like streams through the landscape.

The sheer size of the application and the dramatic effect it would have on the local villages are, in the propaganda released by the developers, points in its favour. It will create employment and bring prosperity. New roads, landscaping and tree planting would be thrown in to make it more politically acceptable.

Those who object say that the plan is inconsistent with most local planning policies: there would be a massive increase in traffic and pollution and the Park's status as an internationally important wildlife habitat would be permanently compromised. The character of the place would be lost for ever.

It is a classic conflict between those who believe that development should be properly planned and of the highest possible standard and those whose business is to exploit and develop the most economic and desirable sites and make the fastest possible return. It is a confrontation which is being mirrored all over the south of England. Occasionally a group of residents has sufficient resources to take a professional, aggressive approach, raise funds and fight the developers on their own terms. Sometimes they win. But even then it is a costly and heartbreaking affair.

Wherwell, Hampshire

Opposite, top An unmetalled country lane before motor transport dominated, Binfield Heath, Oxfordshire, 1910; *bottom* Silchester Common, North Hampshire – the thin heathland soils, of little use for farming, now support conifer plantations

A kitchen garden, Hambleden, Buckinghamshire

Kent

LINDA McCARTNEY's eloquent images of the Weald and the North Downs show the county in all its rural beauty. Her distress at the rapid changes in the Kent and Sussex countryside has been reflected in her efforts to highlight problems such as oil exploration and bad agricultural practices. She is particularly concerned that change in the south-east should be properly considered and development should be controlled and of the best quality. Her landscapes are exhibited all over the world and in recent years she has become closely involved in the conservation movement in general and CPRE in particular.

IT IS EASY TO BE EMOTIONAL ABOUT KENT. Of all the home counties, it has most claim to its own identity. Not only is it the Garden of England, rich in orchards and hop fields, but it is also the rampart of our island kingdom, the only part of the British Isles which can be seen from a foreign shore.

Millions who have returned home from time spent overseas during war and peacetime have stood on ferry decks and looked at the looming coast emerging from the mist. The White Cliffs are more than just a stretch of Heritage Coastline, they are the symbol of homecoming and a safe landfall, the landmark over which Spitfires rose from Biggin Hill and the haven for the little Dunkerque flotillas. It is no wonder that the wounds which have been inflicted on the rich green fabric of the county in recent years have angered so many.

The arrival of the Channel Tunnel has already had a far-reaching and dramatic effect on the future development of Kent. Because of the methods used to make it law the Channel Tunnel Bill has also coloured the public perception of the planning process and cast severe doubt on the use of private bills to shortcut decisions about major developments.

If Great Britain is to play her full role in the European market, the problems of communication with Europe must be solved. The Tunnel will theoretically allow us to travel between London and Paris in two and a half hours by providing a high-speed rail link between the two cities. It will also attract into Kent industry and commerce keen to compete in the European arena, which will in turn require an infrastructure compatible with rapid commercial development.

In a very few years, therefore, Kent will need new rail links and terminals, an improved motorway and trunk road network, industrial and science park developments, warehousing and enough new houses to accommodate the migration of a large work-force into the county. By the end of the century this beautiful, quintessentially English shire could house the new industrial heartland of Britain.

The political presentation of the project now appears to

have been superficial and economical with the facts, and those who know and love Kent feel disillusioned.

The Government believes that the Tunnel will contribute to the prosperity of the entire United Kingdom. Because it is privately financed it must produce a return on investment. Additionally, the project is subject to a treaty with France and must therefore be completed within an agreed timetable. The planning procedures in France are short and even with a major inquiry it is unlikely to take more than six months before a decision is announced on a development. In Britain, a public inquiry into the Channel Tunnel could have taken many years and, the Government argued, made the project unworkable before the end of the century. In the intervening years the delay would have blighted property and had a detrimental effect on our image in the community, and the project would have been unlikely to attract sufficient investment.

The Tunnel Act was therefore authorised by Parliament, with all the limitations on third party access and discussion time that Parliamentary procedures imply. When it was passing through Parliament, the Transport Secretary stated that the existing rail network would suffice. No mention was made of a new high-speed route, one of the principal reasons why a previous scheme in the 1970s was rejected. The Tunnel was presented as a benign development which would result in an improved system of trunk roads. After all, it would obviously be unsatisfactory if beautiful Kent villages were subjected to juggernauts speeding through their lanes. There would have to be an international rail depot at Ashford and freight sidings at the Tunnel mouth and there would be a certain amount of unavoidable development in the countryside near the Tunnel. But this would be counterbalanced by the prosperity which would come to Ashford and Folkestone. The impression was given that, once the decision had been made to go ahead, a certain amount of disruption was inevitable but this would be transitory and confined to small, clearly defined areas. Generally, the Tunnel was characterised as being environmentally

Bethersden, 3 miles from Pluckley – an agricultural village, with a church of Kentish ragstone

Left Magpie Bottom, Shoreham

Kent

Oasthouse, south of Hollingbourne

[78]

Kentish hop country: a block of traditional oasthouses (now replaced by electric kilns), and the hop fields of Hopfield Farm, Mereworth

acceptable and it was suggested that in the long term the attractive character of the Kent countryside would be safeguarded.

It is hardly surprising that the subsequent announcement by British Rail of a new high-speed track designed to carry the French-style 186-miles-per-hour trains created anguish and anger throughout the county. Conveniently revised traffic forecasts, produced by the promoters, suggested that the new rail capacity was vital to the success of the Tunnel. But British Rail's route proposals, initially drawn up on greaseproof paper by a project manager in his kitchen, took only engineering considerations into account, and scythed their way through some of the most beautiful Kent countryside.

The public anger was caused not only by the prospect of the appalling environmental damage through the physical impact of the system, or by the threat of the consequential development of new stations but also by the ineptitude of British Rail's presentation of the case. It appeared to the residents of Kent that their county had been given away to a group of arrogant madmen who were answerable to nobody.

The groups opposed to the route eventually proposed by British Rail agree that more rail capacity is needed but do not believe that the least damaging route has yet been found. They see no convincing argument that the high-speed rail link will lead to a net environmental and economic improvement for the country as a whole. The evidence shows that this insufficiently planned project will lead to relocation of industry away from the regions which need it most and into Kent's overheated economy.

The already strained road network could well be forced to bear the brunt of the freight traffic because the train preferred by British Rail cannot carry it. Neither can the existing British network carry continental wagons because of our narrow tunnel gauge.

The route chosen by British Rail still holds many environmental uncertainties and, whichever solution is eventually found, the effect of the Tunnel on Kent will continue to be a major political issue. CPRE has become closely involved with the campaign, leading the defence on a national basis and working locally with the Kent Trust for Nature Conservation.

Meanwhile, many who live in idyllic villages along the proposed route are protesting that it threatens to obliterate their houses. Delegations of protesters have been to France and measured the sound level of the proposed trains, reporting back with horror stories of a noise like a jet aircraft roaring by every six minutes. Residents of historic houses and ancient villages sheltering under the North Downs are bracing themselves for their toughest struggles since the Battle of Britain. Entire communities have marched on the House of Commons and pressure groups have sprouted into life all over the county. When the decisions have been made and the route constructed, the character of Kent will have been fundamentally changed and many people living in the English countryside will never again feel as secure as they did before the Tunnel was built.

Other problems consequential upon the Tunnel are already beginning to appear. For instance, it is hard to imagine a more absurd or insensitive place to build a four-lane dual carriageway than the top of the White Cliffs of Dover, although this has been promoted by the Department of Transport.

The road would form half of a 9-mile link between the Tunnel terminal and Dover Western Docks. It would run from Court Wood on the A20 across the crest of Shakespeare Cliff and alongside the ancient South Downs Way.

CPRE, the National Trust and the Countryside Commission are all against the proposal. Dover District Council, however, worried about the impact of the Tunnel on local employment, support the idea. They have acknowledged the fearful damage the road will do to the Dover–Folkestone Heritage Coastline but have justified their attitude with the immortal words: 'We're prepared to pay an environmental price if necessary.'

The alternative – a tunnel to the docks under the Western Heights together with improvements to the

White Mill, Headcorn

Left The cliffs between Folkestone and Dover

Under the North Kent Downs – areas threatened by the proposed high-speed rail link between the Channel Tunnel and London

Timber wagon – Kent traditionally produced timber for houses, smock windmills and granaries. The managed woodland remains essential to the Kent landscape.

existing A20 – has been dismissed by the Department of Transport on the grounds of cost.

The Government, notwithstanding its professed environmental concern, has given its blessing to this monstrous venture. The White Cliffs of Dover will henceforth be embellished by the glitter of countless HGV windscreens in the day and headlights at night. The Government and Dover District Council may be prepared to 'pay an environmental price' but the White Cliffs belong to the nation and are close to its heart.

The Tunnel controversy has also coincided with the Kent structure plan debate and the two are now fundamentally linked. CPRE is a fervent supporter of the structure plan as a means of ensuring that necessary development takes place to the right standard and in the appropriate place. It must balance the competing interests of urban and rural areas. The dangers of free-for-all development are obvious but structure plan procedures allow all parties to discuss the County Council's recommendations before they are finalised. The plans which will take Kent into the next century are the most significant in its history.

In its recommendations, however, the County Council enthusiastically supported the case for more development, attempted to weaken the protection of the Green Belt and encouraged the release of green field sites for industrial and domestic building. Some of the proposals went against Government guidance aimed at discouraging the view of London as a source of population and jobs for other areas. There was little reference to any increase in urban-land redevelopment and the revitalisation of the capital's neglected inner city areas.

CPRE believes that Kent can play a role in regenerating such areas by encouraging restraint over development of London's Green Belt fringes. This would protect the countryside and discourage migration outwards from the capital. The County Council's draft plan would have weakened restraint policies in the county and appears to set Kent in competition with not only London but also other counties in the south-east. CPRE feels that national economic growth is best served by creating local structure plans which complement each other in seeking a national objective.

CPRE summarises the plan as tilting all policies in favour of development, making grandiose allocations of land for development and weakening safeguards which have so far protected the countryside. The Secretary of State for the Environment looks set to scotch many of the proposals for relaxing Green Belt controls, but is nevertheless intent on pressing ahead with substantial development that will put huge pressure on the countryside around towns such as Maidstone and Dartford.

The rapid metamorphosis of this beautiful shire has now generated a momentum which will take it, bewildered, into the twenty-first century. There seems to be no doubt that the citizens of Kent will prosper and reap the benefits of Britain's membership of the European market. But for many, the orchards will become little more than the briefest memory as the flying train howls on its arrow-straight line to London.

Hauling timber near Edenbridge, Kent, soon after the end of the First World War

Close to the proposed rail route, near Maidstone

The Sheffield Green Belt and the Peak District National Park

PATRICK LICHFIELD's arresting photographs show the unique beauty of the Peak District. The struggle to protect this wild and rugged landscape, tucked into the heart of industrial England, is one of the most inspiring stories in the conservation movement. That the struggle has been largely successful can be seen from the photographic comparisons between the old and the new. Lord Lichfield is an active and enthusiastic member of CPRE and knows and loves the Peak District National Park.

THE PEAK DISTRICT is an oasis of wild countryside in the centre of England. Surrounded by industrial cities and motorways, it is a vital green lung for Sheffield, Derby, Rotherham, Manchester, Huddersfield and Stoke, and is easily accessible to the seventeen million people who live within 50 miles of its boundaries. The Peak District National Park straddles six counties and is made up of two distinct landscapes. To the south are the deep dales and stone-walled fields of the White Peak. This pleasant and rich agricultural area is surrounded on two sides and to the north by the massive expanse of the Dark Peak with its precipitous gritstone edges and high heather moorland.

The Park is, in some respects, the cradle of the modern landscape conservation movement. In 1932, five men were imprisoned after a mass trespass on Kinder Scout. Their historic protest showed how access to most of the wild stretches of moorland between Manchester and Sheffield was restricted by the landowners. In the massive area between the two cities there were only twelve public footpaths over 2 miles long and the estates were maintained almost exclusively for private grouse-shooting, which was available only to the privileged few. The confrontation between the keepers of the land and the public who were demanding more access marked the end of an era and was one of the root causes of the eventual formation of England's National Parks.

Today, although an absolute right of free access within the Peak District has never been achieved, much of the moorland has been opened up to the public, often after the signing of agreements between landowners and the Park Authority. The Duke of Devonshire was one of the first to cooperate and limited access to the Chatsworth estate was granted in 1935. Since then, large areas of moorland have been acquired by the Park Authority and the National Trust for the combined purposes of increasing public access and improving management.

In the early 1930s the privately-owned landscape had virtually no statutory protection and when it came under threat the only guaranteed solution was to acquire the land. The National Trust now owns 35,000 acres of the

High Peak scenery: Howden Moors

Kinder Scout, from Bradfield

Derwent Edge

Opposite Edale Moor – Kinder Scout in the distance, badly eroded by acid rain, people and sheep, is now the subject of major restoration work by its owner, the National Trust, and by the Peak Park Planning Board

Winnats Pass – CPRE fought off a proposal for a major road widening scheme here in 1939

Peak District and many of the early acquisitions were covenanted or donated to them by CPRE. Ethel Gallimore, daughter of the steel magnate Thomas Ward and later married to the great environmental campaigner Gerald Haythornthwaite, started the Sheffield and Peak District Branch of CPRE. By 1931 it had bought one of the Duke of Rutland's estates, which it handed over to the National Trust – the first large landholding to be owned by the Trust in the area. The branch went on to buy farms in Derbyshire and the Peak District, which were all subsequently given to the National Trust. Today, now that some safeguards against bad development are enshrined in law, CPRE concentrates its efforts on campaigning, leaving land acquisition to other organisations.

The challenge posed in the Peak Park by poor land management and 'reclamation' is significant. Footpaths need to be created and restored, buildings renovated in the vernacular manner, woodlands and heathlands properly managed, stone walls maintained and rebuilt, heather properly burnt and new habitats created. When the Kinder Estate was eventually acquired by the National Trust in 1982, it was in appalling condition, generally run down, overgrazed and polluted. The Trust's restoration of the land, carried out under a joint scheme with the Peak Park Authority's Planning Board, has become a blueprint for management for eventual public access.

The Peak District is one of the busiest and most popular National Parks in Britain and requires constant management and care to maintain and protect it from the stresses and strains of around twenty million annual visitors. Its strategic position in the heart of the industrial north Midlands has predictably made it vulnerable to exploitation from all quarters but most particularly, in recent years, from the leisure industry.

It is fashionable to present leisure with a theme nowadays and large-scale theme park developments such as Alton Towers, close to the western boundary of the Park, have had their effect. North-West Water, having achieved a foot in the door with permission for a single speed-boat on Bottoms reservoir at Tintwhistle, applied for permission to build a vast water-based activity centre on the reservoir, complete with a dry ski-slope and a range of other on-shore facilities. The scale and concept of the development was totally out of place in the Park, and although the application was rejected, the fact that it was made in the first place is indicative of the pressures now being applied by leisure entrepreneurs.

CPRE maintains a close interest in the Peak District and was influential in negotiating its National Park designation. It was the first area to be given this status after the Hobhouse Committee recommendations were formalised in the National Park and Access to the Countryside Act of 1949. Its boundaries had been mapped out as early as 1937 by a group of voluntary bodies, including CPRE, known as the Voluntary Joint Committee of the Peak District National Park. John Dower, who was appointed by the Minister of Town and Country Planning to produce a report on the theory and practice of National Park Policy, came to the area and found that much of his work had already been done for him. Apart from 100 square miles in the south, the Peak District boundaries were agreed, and on 17 April 1951 the Park officially came into being.

CPRE is historically one of the major environmental influences in the area, having one of its busiest and largest branches in Sheffield. Its efforts were crowned with the designation of the Sheffield Green Belt, which stopped the city sprawling out to the west and allowed controlled development in less sensitive areas.

The Green Belt issue had come to a head after a plan to build ninety houses in beautiful countryside at Whirlow Bridge was thrown out by Sheffield City Council, who were then forced to pay compensation to the builder. CPRE then presented its recommendations for the Green Belt and was asked to produce a detailed survey of the countryside surrounding the city which should be given protection and form a buffer to development. Though a provisional Green Belt was quickly approved by the Council in 1938, it was not formally adopted until 1983, after forty-five years of campaigning.

Upper Ouzelden Clough, a site of afforestation between the wars

Winnats Pass

Hallam Moors from Whinstone Lee Tor

Today the Peak District National Park covers an area of 542 square miles, of which around half is enclosed farmland, and over a third open moorland. It supports a permanent population of 38,000 and the main settlements are Bakewell, Tideswell, Castleton and Hathersage. The Peak District is essentially a people's Park and it is enjoyed to the full by millions of those who live within reach of its borders. It is possible to be rock climbing on Stanage Edge less than twenty minutes after leaving the centre of Sheffield.

The appearance of the landscape has been profoundly influenced by farming. The Dark Peak is mostly given over to sheep while to the south are small, predominantly dairy farms. For generations stone buildings and walls have given a balance and beauty to the manmade elements of the farmed countryside. Today, however, all is not well. As in the Lake District, the difficulties and costs of maintenance have resulted in dry stone walls falling into disrepair in many parts of the Park with the consequential loss of ancient field patterns. Overgrazing in the moors of the Dark Peak is becoming a serious problem. A survey commissioned by CPRE in 1980 showed that land stripped of all vegetation was being eroded. In the south, wetlands have been drained, and in the White Peak hay meadows have been used to produce silage. Wild flowers have been sprayed out of existence. Ugly modern agricultural buildings have appeared in increasing numbers and the landscape is changing gradually for the worse. This is a nettle which has been grasped by the Park Authority in its experiments in sympathetically designed rural development. More recently, through the Government's initiative in recognising the Dark Peak as an Environmentally Sensitive Area, efforts are at last being made which will benefit the landscape, wildlife and appearance of the Park.

The physical demonstrations of the 1930s may have ceased, but there have since been many battles instigated by those who wanted to exploit the beauty of the Park or expand the industrial potential of the adjacent cities.

A major test came in 1955 when plans were announced to build a Grand Prix motor-racing track around the

Coldwall Bridge, Dovedale – land acquired by the National Trust between the wars

Opposite, top Traditional farmstead: The Pond, Peak Forest; *bottom* Inter-war ribbon development along the roads out of Sheffield sparked off a CPRE campaign which led to the designation of the Sheffield Green Belt

Rushup Edge

Near Castleton

The original site of the seventeenth-century Derwent Packhorse Bridge was submerged by the Ladybower reservoir. The local CPRE branch dismantled it before the Second World War, and in 1959 re-erected it at Slippery Stones.

top of Dovedale above Hartington. The plan was defeated after CPRE mobilised massive press and public resistance. In 1963 the CEGB applied to install a power line over the Longdendale Valley and the Woodhead Pass. CPRE objected vigorously and the power lines were rerouted down an old rail track and through tunnels.

A more serious threat was the Manchester to Sheffield motorway which was proposed in 1977. Photography was used by the objectors to show the appalling damage which would have been done to the Park and the idea was eventually dropped, though it has re-emerged in a revised form in the Department of Transport's 1989 Roads White Paper.

Other problems, particularly those of mineral extraction, have also proved less easy to dismiss. Mining is a big industry in the Peak District where there are around 360 sites employing around 10 per cent of the local population. There are valuable deposits of limestone and around 80 per cent of the outcrop running through Derbyshire and Staffordshire lies in the Park. Mining was carried out here long before it became a National Park and the ugly scars of the quarries can be seen at Eldon Hill near Castleton and at Tunstead, near the Park boundary at Buxton, where there is a vast face. These great white wounds on the landscape are visible for miles and the filth, noise and traffic which the quarries have generated is completely incompatible with the ideals of National Parks.

The Government has said that mineral extraction from the National Parks must be demonstrated to be in the country's interest – the operators of both Eldon Hill and Topley Pike recently failed to justify extension of their activities beyond the end of the century following opposition by statutory and voluntary bodies alike. But the industry is powerful and unlikely to take these defeats lying down. Quarrying could be a problem for a long time to come.

But it was the implications of water privatisation which most alarmed the defenders of the Peak District. North-west Water owns 80 square miles – 15 per cent – of the Park, and is by far the biggest landowner. There are access restrictions on much of this acreage which is some of the wildest and most beautiful in the area. The Longdendale Valley with its five reservoirs is entirely owned by the Water Authority.

Despite amendments to the Water Act that it secured in Parliament, CPRE feels that the new water companies will have different aspirations for their land assets than their predecessors. Branch Secretary Elizabeth Garland confirms that CPRE will be watching like a hawk to ensure that the hard-won concessions are implemented in the Parks, and that the water companies themselves are not tempted to become developers.

Land around Lode Mill, Dovedale, owned by the National Trust

Sharplow Dale, part of Dovedale

Opposite Ladybower reservoir surrounded by Hope Forest and Howden Moors

Dartmoor

Denis Waugh's luminous images of Dartmoor were taken in the wet winter months when black clouds skim across the tors and sudden sunlight miraculously transforms the harsh grey crags and the sodden heathland. Waugh learnt the fundamentals of his craft in his native New Zealand and came to England in 1970. He has since travelled the world as a commercial and editorial photographer. 'I have always loved the English landscape and one of the reasons I work hard is so that I can spend more time on the land.'

'Dartmoor is a huge panorama of wide skies and endless, lonely horizons. It is essentially English in its beauty and every time I come away from it I am haunted with the desire to protect it.'

Dartmoor is one of the few corners of Britain where it is still possible to enjoy the mantle of total solitude. It is an elemental place where water, rock, earth and sky combine to create a timeless, savagely beautiful landscape. Although it lies close to a busy coastal resort area, it contains some of the wildest and most inhospitable countryside in the British Isles.

In 1951 Dartmoor became England's fourth National Park and at 233,000 acres, or 365 square miles, is one of the smallest. Fifty-two per cent of Dartmoor is moorland and 35 per cent is farmed. There is a small acreage of woodland and forest. The permanent population is around thirty thousand, although eight million tourists visit the moor every year and there are over 460 miles of footpaths and bridleways to cater for them.

Tourist Dartmoor is the ponies, the prison and the wide, open, rock-strewn spaces. The prison remains one of the most powerful images of the Park and to come across it, solid and austere, in the wet winter mist is still a depressing, uncomfortable experience. Princetown is a grey place at the best of times and the prison is an anachronism in modern society. It is as if this sad, granite-bound community has been left to us by our ancestors as a warning.

Like the other National Parks, Dartmoor generates strong passions, particularly in the breasts of those who know and love the place yet are afraid for its safety. In 1986, many fears were realised when, after years of bitter debate, a road was driven through the northern edge of the Park to the south of Okehampton. Having degenerated into an infamous and acrimonious dispute between environmentalists and the narrow interests of farming and politics, the fight to route Okehampton's bypass away from the Park was first won and then almost immediately lost – after an extraordinary series of political machinations in which the farm lobby was noticeably active, the Secretary of State, Nicholas Ridley, overrode the decision of his Parliamentary Select Committee and allowed the road to be built through the Park. 'Anyone who disagrees that this was the best environmental decision is a

Lustleigh, a village to the east of Dartmoor

Looking towards Widecombe in the Moor, 1948

High on the moor

Clapper bridge

Dunnabridge Pound,
Lydford, Devon, 1902

In the heart of the moor

fanatic,' he said afterwards in a television interview, dismissing the feelings of many of his own party. So the road was eventually finished in 1988 and the ancient deer park under Okehampton castle was riven in two. The people of Okehampton must be relieved that the traffic jams which plagued them for so many years have gone, but many mourn the loss of the peaceful old park and the bluebell woods, bequeathed to the people of the town by Mrs Ryan in memory of her daughter.

The most dominant feature of Dartmoor is the exposed mass of granite, some 1,200 feet high, which forms a broad, rolling upland. It is drained to the south by the headwaters and tributaries of the Rivers Tavy, Avon, Dart and Teign and in the north by the Taw and the Okement.

After a cloudburst, the water races in torrents from the high peaks, swelling the becks and roaring over the granite. Water is everywhere on the moor and the light invests the tumbling streams, ponds and mires with a luminous intensity. The Dartmoor rainstorms can be ferocious and all-consuming, whipped to a fury by the westerlies thundering and howling across the moors from the Atlantic coastline.

Granite tors are scattered all over Dartmoor, ground by the weather into soft, rounded, sometimes hollowed out shapes, or tumbling untidily down the slopes. In the bleak, wild northern heights they sprout like stone mushrooms from moorland rising to over 2,000 feet. This upland is mostly bog and wet heath and is grazed by wild ponies, cattle and sheep. There is little tree cover apart from a few commercial plantations and three areas of stunted oak woodland in the centre of the moor, and there are few settlements. Remains of ancient forest found preserved in bog and peat show that Dartmoor was once covered in trees and that they were cleared by man as he settled on the moor and started to farm.

Wistman's Wood between Beardown and Lynch Tor is composed of mature oaks. Twisted into strange tortured shapes, the trees have taken root amongst lichen-covered granite boulders. Many are at least four hundred years old

Widecombe Fair, established in the Middle Ages, was still a mainly agricultural event in the inter-war period

Dartmoor

Looking towards
Widecombe in the Moor

Sheep are grazed on the
bleak uplands

Providence
hamlet

and the wood is probably a relic of the forest which once covered the moor.

The lowlands surrounding the central granite plateau are of Devonian and Carboniferous age. As they have become eroded they have formed steep slopes and deep valleys and ravines. These areas contain oaks which once formed the basis of a coppice industry and the valleys are lush and green, echoing with the torrents draining from the plateau above.

The eastern fringe of Dartmoor is gentle and settled and contains more agricultural land. The old villages such as Buckland in the Moor and Drewsteignton, where the thatched cottages are still traditionally built of granite or cob, have great charm and have for the most part kept their character.

China clay is still worked on the south-western fringe of the Park and there are abandoned tin workings in many places. Granite was mined here in Victorian times and close to Haytor the remains of a mine have been preserved. The tram-lines which were used to carry the stone to the canal and then down to Teignmouth were themselves carved from granite and are still as good as new. London Bridge, Nelson's Column and New Scotland Yard were all built with Dartmoor stone, often hewn from the land by convicts or prisoners of war.

Stone quarried from the moor is still used in road construction and as ballast by British Rail, which owns Meldon quarry near Okehampton. Quarrying is an important local industry and Meldon is now one of the largest quarries in Britain. It is vital to the local economy and the construction industry, and its importance has meant that those concerned with the environmental integrity of Dartmoor have for many years kept a close eye on it. British Rail has announced plans to sell the quarry and there is much concern that a new commercial owner would increase the mineral extraction beyond an acceptable level. One day Meldon will no longer be viable and will be returned to some sort of natural state. It is then that the voracious construction industry would be forced to look elsewhere – and the moor is rich in minerals.

Huccaby Bridge

Opposite Fingle Bridge

Beneath the granite tors the lowland is lush and green

Combestone Tor

View down the valley from Combestone Tor

The china clay extraction from Dartmoor's south-west fringes has turned this area into an eerie lunar landscape. CPRE and the Dartmoor Preservation Association have fought for years to prevent further encroachment on to Lee Moor, an outpost of Dartmoor which stands proudly on what is otherwise a scene of devastation. It was the Dartmoor Park Authority which in 1988 succeeded in bringing about a major ruling which could help the whole of Britain. Operators are now being told that minerals may be removed but only in the national interest and only if the landscape is scrupulously returned to its former state.

The Army has long been associated with Dartmoor, where it practises its arts and trains its recruits. Military occupation extends to around 33,000 acres, mostly towards the north and the west and including much of the highest moorland. Firing and manoeuvres are signified by red flags hoisted on the hills, snapping in the breeze. Sometimes walkers are briefly allowed to roam on the forbidden acres and they find the tors littered with the spent cartridges and shell cases of mock battles. It is hard to imagine a harsher or more inhospitable place to learn the art of war. The Park Authority has a constant struggle to limit the crater damage caused by live shelling and the digging of slit trenches by the infantry.

CPRE has long held that military training is incompatible with the objectives of the National Parks. But the Army has camped here since 1870, when the War Office first leased some land from the Duchy of Cornwall. Today the military foot remains firmly in the door and the Government shows no inclination to change the existing arrangements. There are some who believe that the Army occupation has in fact been beneficial and has meant that the moor has, for the most part, been left in its natural state, unaffected by pressures of tourism. But the increasing sophistication of military hardware and its potential for damage to the landscape is a serious and escalating problem.

The only signs here in the seemingly endless military grounds are the intrusive warnings against encroaching on Army land. Nevertheless, this is still the real wild Dartmoor which, at some future date, could become public property – it would be a crime to tame it.

The five Dartmoor rivers are born at Cranmere Pool between Hangingstone Hill and Great Kneeset. They go their separate ways, fed by countless streams, swilling over the grit and granite, forming pools for the brown trout and flashing into flood after the storm. They pass through valleys and woods of great beauty on the way to their estuaries and the ever-present wetness attracts a varied and abundant wildlife. Every corner of the moor is embellished with a stream or a river but there are no large lakes other than those which have been created by man. The demand for water in the large urban populations around the Park has resulted in the creation of eight reservoirs, including two new lakes at Avon Dam and Meldon built since the end of the Second World War. There has been steady pressure, so far resisted, to increase abstraction of water – in the early 1970s Parliament refused permission for a new reservoir at Swincombe.

The high plateaus are common grazing land and the winter feeding practices adopted by farmers have begun to cause heavy damage to the areas of heathland. The earth is often poisoned by the indiscriminate dumping of silage and the high moors are churned and hacked by tractors. The scars are signs of the times: the working day for the Dartmoor farmer is long and hard and there are few young people willing to saddle a horse and set out cross-country when a warm tractor is waiting outside the farm door.

As in all National Parks, the Dartmoor Park Authority has little control over the actual landscape. Until recent years it has been unable to help sustain the patterns of farming which are its very essence. The 1986 Dartmoor Commons Act gives a basis for managing the 38,000 hectares of common land on the moor. At the same time it improves access and supports traditional hill-farming in the Park.

The harsh environment of the moor and the struggle for survival applies to the land as well as the creatures which frequent it. Dartmoor is our children's sanctuary. It must be kept carefully for them.

Clapper bridge

Old tramway by Haytor – the mine which it served is now disused

Opposite, top The military road near Okehampton; *bottom* The Okehampton bypass

Exmoor

BRIAN HARRIS is one of the finest practitioners of landscape photography working in the British media. He is a full-time staff photographer at the *Independent*, a newspaper which has pioneered a massive improvement in the standard of half-tone reproduction. Harris's delicate and subtle images are notable for their power to communicate and his work has attracted widespread praise, not only from the public but from his peers. He travels extensively for his paper and covered the French and the American elections in 1988; he is familiar with the difficulties of working to tight deadlines and the problems of achieving a good picture in bad conditions.

This was his first visit to Exmoor and his impressions of a moorland landscape which has suffered great change at the hand of man are powerful and to the point.

Opposite, top View across Riscombe and the Exe Valley; *bottom* The Barle Valley near Simonsbath. River valleys cut deep into the cultivated plateau of Exmoor – their steep slopes are little used and are often wooded.

EXMOOR STRADDLES THE COUNTIES of Devon and Somerset and was made a National Park in 1954. It is rich in traces of ancient civilisation and, like Dartmoor, was extensively settled by Bronze Age man. Remains of their barrows, stone circles and burial mounds are common, particularly in the moorland north of Challacombe. The early settlers cleared and farmed the higher land until they learnt to exploit the thickly-wooded lowlands and began to desert the moor. There are over one hundred mediaeval settlements on Exmoor, many associated with mining. They are signs of a busy and often prosperous past spanning many hundreds of years. There is evidence of iron age hill forts, Norman fortresses and nineteenth-century iron and copper mining. Today new sites are regularly unearthed, and it is only recently that the archaeological importance of Exmoor has been understood.

From Norman times until the early nineteenth century, Exmoor was a royal forest where deer and wild boar were hunted and cattle were grazed. But enclosure legislation stopped all that and in 1815 the character of the moor was changed almost overnight as boundaries were laid down and farmers eyed the land. Dartmoor survived the enclosures almost untouched but its smaller, more manageable neighbour changed fundamentally, both in appearance and use. The wet soggy peat bog was gradually improved and farmed and the process of damage to the rich archaeological heritage began.

By 1917 the old hunting forest had been reduced in size to 20,000 acres. It was then acquired by John Knight, a business man, who hoped that he would be able to enclose it and grow crops. In his enthusiasm he opened up Exmoor, built settlements and roads across the moorland, divided the land and planted the beech hedges which survive to this day. The experiment was the first attempt by modern man at 'reclaiming' Exmoor for agricultural use and, while it was not a success, it laid the foundations for future, more successful projects. Between 1947 and 1977, 20 per cent of Exmoor's moorland was appropriated for more intensive agriculture, and also for forestry. With the aid of grants and incentives the old wilderness of heather and bog was drained, fenced in, sowed with rye grass, fertilised, sprayed with pesticides, ploughed, planted and bullied into the uniform, efficient but characterless features of the modern agribusiness estates. Even at 10,000 feet, intensive sheep rearing and sometimes even arable farming took over from Exmoor's traditional form of management. It became obvious that, unless something was done, Exmoor was in danger of losing all its traditional moorland, and National Park designation would be little more than an expensive farce.

Exmoor was given National Park status because, in 1947, 60,000 acres of the Park were a unique and valuable mixture of coastal heaths, grass moorland and heather moors. Government subsidies to farmers to increase output resulted in this unique landscape dwindling to 48,000 acres in less than twenty years. Farming had always been a fundamental part of Exmoor life, from the arable and dairy farming on the rich alluvial soil around Porlock to the extensive rearing of livestock on the moors. But formerly there was a balance, more accidental than designed, between the value of the moor as an amenity and its use as a source of revenue. In the years between 1947 and 1977, Government policy completely upset the balance.

The resulting outcry and debate in which CPRE and the Exmoor Society were prominent led to the Porchester Report of 1977. This recommended that Exmoor should be surveyed and all remaining areas of traditional moor or heath defined. The report suggested that two maps should be created. They would show the locations of the remaining moorland and within it those areas which should be preserved for all time. In the pre-eminent area encircling Dunkery Beacon and the heartland of the moor, agricultural improvement was to be banned. This policy was to be enforced with Moorland Conservation Orders issued by the Park Authority. Every application to farm moorland would be closely examined and compensation paid on a 'once and for all' basis to the farmer if his application was rejected.

Looking west across the
moor above Weatherslade

A foxhunt near Tarr Steps

The beach at Bossington
looking east towards
Hurlstone Point

View west across Withypool

Hanging Water at Woody Bay

In the end, little of the Porchester Report was taken up. Critical areas were identified and mapped but the Park Authority was never granted the power to impose conservation orders. All that were eventually effected were voluntary management agreements between the farmers and the Authority. The farmers were to be compensated every year for what they would have earned by ruining the landscape. The watering-down of the report was an indication of the power of the farming lobby and has resulted in ludicrous claims based on spurious estimates of revenue from the wilderness. Agreements have gradually been finalised between landowners and the Park Authority, which receives 90 per cent of the cost from the Government. However only one-third of the critical land on the second map, the heartland, has so far been protected in this way.

The example of Exmoor was followed by the Government in drafting the Wildlife and Countryside Act of 1981, although the principle of 'lost profits' compensation remains a problem in the Act's implementation. Despite the withdrawal of many improvement grants and a downturn in agricultural fortunes, which have taken the pressure off moorland 'reclamation', the problems of ensuring good moorland management seem intractable. A typical example is Winsford Hill, which it is generally agreed should be granted the status of an SSSI. The National Trust has negotiated a ninety-nine-year lease although it has no control over grazing rights which have been retained by the freeholder. There is no management agreement and the land has been, and continues to be, seriously overgrazed. While all the concerned bodies wallow in bureaucracy, nothing is done, the problem becomes worse and the heather continues to disappear.

Exmoor is made up of 265 square miles of moorland, exceptionally valuable woodland and farmland. It has a population of around ten thousand of which about two thousand work on the land. Over half the land area is given over to cattle and sheep with a little mixed farming in the wooded river valleys. The 29 miles of coastline are one of the most important features of the Park and are protected by the Park Authority and the National Trust, and by their own inaccessibility. The rugged cliffs are havens for puffins, razorbills, kittiwakes, Manx shearwaters and cormorants as well as herring gulls by the million. The cliffs are crowned in places by dense and ancient oak woodland and occasionally broken by deep valleys and waterfalls.

The deciduous woodland covers almost 8,000 acres and is concentrated in the river valleys, along the coast and on the north-facing slopes of the Brendon Hills. It is part of the glory of the Park but has suffered badly from lack of management and the encroachment of rhododendrons which inhibit regeneration and choke the woodland floor. The Park Authority owns over 1,000 acres which are subject to its woodland plan, and it is trying to negotiate voluntary management agreements in areas where it considers woodland is at risk. Forestry Commission plantations cover around 3,500 acres and the Commission cooperates with the Park Authority to agree afforestation policy.

In common with Dartmoor, rainwater runs swiftly from Exmoor, a characteristic which has been exaggerated by the numerous drainage schemes which have steadily reduced the area of wetland and mire. In 1952, after 9 inches of rain fell in only twenty-four hours, the River Lyn burst its banks and flooded Lynmouth, killing thirty-four people. Since then, water management schemes have been introduced and Wimbleball Reservoir was completed in 1981 after a successful but bitter struggle by conservation groups to have it resited from its original planned position at Lanacre on Withypool Common. The former water authority owns 850 acres of Exmoor, and the Exmoor Society, in common with other societies concerned with conserving the National Parks, is worried at the possibility of development on the land.

Exmoor has until recently been less popular in terms of numbers of visitors than other National Parks. However, it is relatively small and comparatively hard to reach. The arrival of the North Devon link-road, which runs straight

The village of Winsford, 1930s

as an arrow from the M5 at Tiverton to Barnstaple, may well change all this. The road was intended to open up North Devon and there are signs that the improved access has already attracted development to the area. A new motor-racing circuit at Drewstone near North Molton is planned 2 miles from the boundary of the moor and there are many examples of housing development on the edge of the Park.

The biggest threat of all, however, is still agricultural damage to Exmoor. While no major ploughing has taken place in recent years, the safety of much of the land identified in the Porchester Report as prime moorland is still not guaranteed. There remains an uneasy, unstable balance between conservation and agriculture on Exmoor.

Exmoor

Looking south-west from Porlock Common across Exmoor Forest

Exmoor

Almsworth Common

Overleaf Looking east across Holnicott
Estate

Hampshire

Clive Arrowsmith is one of the world's finest portrait photographers. He has had a long association with the Council for the Protection of Rural England and his commitment to the countryside was demonstrated in CPRE's Tomorrow project in 1986 with a portfolio of pictures of the countryside subsequently bisected by the notorious North Devon link-road.

His stunning photographs of the New Forest on the edge of Lyndhurst, taken on a single autumn day, were originally commissioned for Legacy but have already been a significant influence in rallying public opinion against the county council's plan to build a badly conceived bypass round the town.

Estate agent law says that your first impression of a place is the one which will stay with you for the rest of your life. So when you first visit Hampshire, make sure that you approach it from Newbury and climb on to the Downs through the villages of Ashmansworth and Faccombe. You will be left with a vision of a sublime, untamed countryside where it is possible to walk for miles without meeting another soul and where, in the wooded valleys and high, windswept Downs, time seems to stand still. You will have left the hi-tech landscapes of modern enterprise behind in Berkshire. Here it is the villages, the small rural communities, the fields and the narrow roads which create the pattern of life.

If, on the other hand, you drive into the county along the M3 motorway, leaving it at Basingstoke, taking a leisurely drive through the new estates and pausing now and again to visit the sprawling clutches of ringroad superstores, you will perhaps feel less sympathetic towards a county which, in spite of much conflict, remains one of the jewels in the crown of south-east England.

Hampshire is the largest shire county and, with the exception of Berkshire, the most threatened by development. The network of motorways and trunk roads has opened it up and exposed its remote corners to us all. The main urban centres are all growing apace and, in the north of the county, developers congregate to lay the foundations of new 'country towns'.

The chalk streams which meander through the heart of Hampshire are among the greatest glories in the county. The Itchen and the Test are holy waters, Meccas for fly fishers from all over the world. But perhaps the richest prize is the New Forest, which is unique in Europe as an ancient and comparatively unspoilt oak forest. Inexplicably, it has not yet been given the status of a National Park although there is a chance that it will be protected in this way before the end of the century.

If the great urban settlements of Aldershot, Basingstoke, Southampton and Portsmouth were to be removed from the shire we would be left with a million acres of farmland, enhanced with soft rolling woodland, and

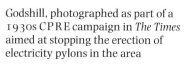

Godshill, photographed as part of a 1930s CPRE campaign in *The Times* aimed at stopping the erection of electricity pylons in the area

Ringwood, on the edge of the New Forest, has expanded greatly since the 1930s, when its population was 5,000

The Test Valley – under the controversial mineral extraction scheme given the go-ahead in 1989, sand and gravel will be carried along conveyor belts near this stretch of river

On the proposed Lyndhurst bypass route through the New Forest: common grazing . . .

. . . a typical lawn

. . . and a view towards Lyndhurst

small villages. In spite of the rapid growth of new industries and new populations to go with them, Hampshire remains a charming, essentially rural county. Its desirability as a place to live is so far uncompromised by the tremendous pressure for development, although there are growing signs of stress in the system. Plans for major new green field settlements which are contrary to the recommendations of the structure plan are regularly submitted and given serious consideration in Whitehall.

Two recent campaigns with which CPRE, in both its local and national capacity, has been involved are an indication of the strife within the county.

It is difficult to imagine a more grotesque threat to the beautiful River Test than that it should be traversed by conveyor belts. But in 1988 Hall Aggregates, a subsidiary of Ready Mixed Concrete, applied to extract around $1\frac{1}{2}$ million tons of sand and hoggin from a 44-acre field on Kimbridge Farm to the south-west of the valley of the River Test.

It is national policy that each area must do its best to be self-sufficient in the supply of minerals. In South Hampshire there is a big deficit of building sand. Some quarries are nearing the end of their lives and must be replaced. The problem is the massive boom in development in the region, particularly around Andover, Chandler's Ford, Southampton and Basingstoke. As development continues to escalate, so does the demand for materials.

Under the proposed Test scheme, the sand would be moved on a mile-long conveyor belt across the river to a dump yard on the A3057 between Stockbridge and Romsey. The belt would run at a height of 1 yard, occasionally rising to 2 yards, and would follow a disused railway line for some of its length. The extraction would take nine years with an average of eighty-eight lorry movements a day.

It is easy to see why the impact of the application was massive and immediate – the water-meadows are rich in flowers and wildlife, and in spring, when the mayfly rises and the hawthorn blossom and the scent of wild garlic and

Lymington River in the New Forest

Opposite, top When *The Times* published this photograph in the 1930s, the Avon Valley in the New Forest was already subject to a conservation campaign against the proposed construction of electricity pylons in the area; *bottom* Gathering Christmas trees on Forestry Commission land between Lyndhurst and Ringwood in the 1930s – Sitka spruce, Corsican pine and European larch were introduced to the New Forest to sustain the commercial forestry of the area

On the route of the proposed Lyndhurst bypass. In 1989 CPRE helped stop new development at the site of Fawley power station (*above*, on the horizon).

The New Forest Association, revived in 1927, aimed to prevent indiscriminate felling in ancient woodland such as Birley Old Wood, and also succeeded in persuading the Forestry Commission to remove seedling firs from open land in the Forest

new life is all around, it is the essence of the English countryside. Even in the late autumn, when the light is slate grey and the valley is drenched and misty, there is enchantment in the air. Small wonder then that public reaction forced the Secretary of State to call the application in, appoint an inspector and make it clear that the final decision would be taken in Whitehall.

A local group was formed to fight the plan. Originally called 'RAPE' but quickly amended to the more delicate 'SAVE', it received support from around the world and attracted a powerful team of patrons including Lord Denning, Sir Thomas Sopwith, Mr Robin Aisher OBE, Sir David Mitchell MP, Mr Michael Colvin MP, Mr Leslie Thomas, Mr David Frost and Mr Norman Thelwell.

Village shops across the valley displayed posters showing the great maw of a digger gouging out the bed of a beautiful river. 'Save the Test Valley. Stop the Gravel Vandals,' it said. Local papers alleged that the pit, once dug, would become a rubbish tip. The local MP said on BBC Radio, 'If you want to see the whole of the Test Valley, from one end to the other, become a monumental gravel pit, then give the go-ahead to this application.'

Much of the propaganda put about by the local pressure group was inaccurate, however. Contrary to its statements, the extraction site was not in an Area of Outstanding Natural Beauty, nor was it a Site of Special Scientific Interest, nor an Environmentally Sensitive Area. There are of course strict controls over mineral extraction. Hampshire County Council would not allow the valley of the Test to be turned into a gravel pit and there was never any question of rubbish being tipped on the site after it had been dug out. Much of the anger of the local residents was consequently misrouted and counter-productive.

CPRE and the more experienced objectors were dismayed by the campaign and distanced themselves from it. Knowing the importance of making accurate and responsible objections which relate to the law, CPRE objected on the grounds of traffic and precedent. The minerals would be removed through a small side road beside Mottisfont, a twelfth-century Augustinian priory on the banks of the

Test which is owned by the National Trust. In any case, it was unacceptable that permission should be given to lay a mile-long conveyor belt across one of the most beautiful and precious river valleys in England. If granted, the mineral-rich valley would immediately become vulnerable to other similar applications. But it was an ingenious suggestion and the developers made their case well.

In the end, Hall Aggregates won their case and the Secretary of State ratified the inspector's recommendation that the plan should be approved subject to the normal safeguards. It is possible that the scheme will cause little damage to the Test Valley. But it is a major precedent and should further applications be made, there is every possibility that conveyor belts will become a familiar sight throughout this glorious vale.

In 1987, to the fury of conservationists everywhere, Hampshire County Council promoted a bill to drive a bypass through the New Forest, close to Lyndhurst. The need for traffic relief was not in dispute: at the height of the season, fourteen thousand cars daily pour through the town's narrow streets. It was the route and the means which the Council used to promote it which many found unacceptable.

To the eight million of us who visit the Forest each year, it is a place for a family day out – somewhere to walk, look at the ponies and take a picnic. It is almost taken for granted. But this stretch of park and woodland is unique and has been so sensitively managed by man that much of the area would be recognisable to Neolithic people. Nowhere else in Europe is there such an extent of ancient countryside. It is a mixture of heathland, oak, beech and holly, and the open 'lawns' or glades which characterise the heart of the forest.

The Nature Conservancy Council estimates that 50 per cent of our old-established woodland has been lost since the Second World War. While the New Forest has suffered and lost some of its character through the pressures of tourism, overgrazing and the invasion of scrub, it has managed to remain relatively intact. It is nevertheless flanked by danger with Southampton and Fawley to the

Near Brockenhurst in the New Forest

Areas threatened by the Lyndhurst bypass proposals. Bolton's Bench (*opposite*), where Forest and town meet, would have been severed from the Forest if the scheme had gone ahead.

In the New Forest

east and Bournemouth to the west. There have been pressures from the oil industry to run pipelines through to Southampton Water and applications to build all sorts of leisure facilities.

The County Council's plan was to drive a $1\frac{3}{4}$-mile route deep into the forest. Eighty acres of woodland would have been cut off from the rest and the effect on the future of the forest and its plant and animal life would have been devastating. The County Council used the device of a private bill to push the project through Parliament. Under the New Forest Act, the plan would otherwise have been presented before the 'Verderer's court', an ancient body given new powers by Parliament specifically for the purpose of protecting the Crown Land of the New Forest from damaging threats. There would have been a public debate which would have gone to arbitration in the case of disagreement. The private bill allowed the Council to make their case to a committee of MPs and to avoid the embarrassment of public confrontation, including the scrutiny of a public inquiry.

The CPRE campaign, in which Clive Arrowsmith's photographs played a prominent part, kept the electorate accurately informed and put the case against the County Council's road and the method which was being used to force the plans through. In the end the select committee of MPs threw the application out, making the point that Hampshire County Council were wrong to have used the private bill to promote their case.

The New Forest Review published in 1988 recommended the setting up of a committee of all the parties involved in the protection of the forest and the strengthening of protection of the Heritage area. In the twenty-first century, voluntary bodies without statutory powers are unlikely to be effective. CPRE believes in a statutory authority with its own budget and a remit to provide the conservation which the forest so badly needs.

Hampshire is a county at the crossroads. Let us hope that those who want to live there can be accommodated in communities in which quality of life and concern for the environment are prime considerations.

Bramshaw Common, New Forest, 1928. Open commons for grazing ponies and cattle intersperse the wooded area. The scattered village of Bramshaw is in one of the tracts of agricultural land, traditionally made up of smallholdings.

The Lyndhurst bypass would have had a devastating effect on a large area of the Forest

The North York Moors

BARRY LATEGAN, an American citizen now resident in England, was born in South Africa in 1935. In 1959 he went to work for the Cape Town photographer Ginger Odes, who started him along the road to professional photography. Lategan continued his training as an assistant in London in the early Sixties. His 1966 photograph of Lesley Hornby, one of the most famous model shots ever taken, launched the waiflike Twiggy on her career.

Lategan's work has been published throughout the world. He has been awarded numerous accolades, notably the 1988 Halina Award for the Pirelli Calendar from the Photographers Gallery in London, British and American Television awards as well as awards from the Association of Fashion, Advertising and Editorial Photographers.

Lategan has developed a close association with the English countryside and is fascinated with the fervent idiosyncrasies of English rural life. 'I was introduced to Yorkshire through the Legacy assignment. May my photographs express my feelings.'

THE NORTH YORK MOORS form the most easterly of the National Parks. They rise dramatically above the Vales of Pickering in the south and York and Mowbray in the west. To the east and north-east is the North Sea. The Park is close to Teesside and the towns of Whitby and Scarborough. It is formed from Jurassic rocks gently folded into a series of domes and basins and overlaid by deposits of thin, acid peat, boulder clay, glacial sands and gravels. The Park's rolling heather moorland – the Cleveland and Hambleton Hills in the west and the North Yorks Moors proper in the east – is the principal reason for the National Park designation. Much of it is managed for grouse-shooting and is extensively grazed by sheep. There are few deciduous trees on the higher ground, though the numerous narrow valleys which dissect the moorland are often well wooded and there are large plantations of conifers in the south-east of the Park, notably Dalby Forest. Towards the Vales of York and Mowbray, the moorland falls sharply, often in precipitous cliffs or 'scars'. To the south-east the descent is more gradual and the moorland is penetrated by a series of broad valleys running from north to south and drained by tributaries of the River Derwent. These valleys, together with the narrow belt of lower land between Helmsley and Thornton Dale, provide good agricultural land which is used both for dairy farming and the growing of cereal crops.

Most of the land is privately owned although the Park Authority and the National Trust have acquired around 10 per cent of the Park and now control some of the most sensitive areas such as the Hole of Horcum and Lockton High Moor. Half the moor is common land.

The North Yorkshire Moors have a dramatic Heritage Coastline with cliffs rising to over 700 feet in places, and there are several picturesque fishing villages. Both ironstone and alum have been worked in the Park in days gone by and the last iron ore mine closed in 1964. Whitby is renowned for jet, a fossil of conifer, which is either collected on the shore or mined, and is used in jewellery. Jet has been mined here since the Bronze Age, and when it was fashionable during the latter part of the nineteenth

Pallet Hill Farm and Kirkby Knowle

Traditional farming and moorland versus intensive agriculture and forestry: near Bransdale/near Gillamoor

Near Rosedale Abbey/Rosedale Moor

Bilsdale from Newby Bank

century nearly two thousand local people were employed in the industry of mining and making it into necklaces and brooches.

There is a working potash mine at Boulby in the north of the Park. Large deposits of the mineral, which is used as an agricultural fertiliser, were discovered during oil exploration and around 300,000 tons are now mined every year. Various applications to extend the mine into the Park have been made and refused on the grounds that they would cause environmental damage. In 1978, after a public inquiry, an appeal by the mine owners was rejected by the Secretary of State.

The passage of history is written on the face of the North Yorkshire Moors. The landscape of the fells is extremely beautiful and the contours, formed by the gentle forces of rain and weather, are distinguished by man's frequent interventions. On the high moorland signs of the antiquity of human occupation – barrows, cairns, long barrows, standing stones and stone circles – are still to be found in profusion on land which has never been wholly tamed by man and has been relatively untouched for 2,500 years. Iron Age man inhabited a wooded landscape which he set about clearing before moving to the lowlands and the coast.

The rich archaeological landscape contains over three hundred sites scheduled as ancient monuments. Bronze Age field patterns and fortifications can be seen on the skyline of the high moors and there was a Roman settlement at Cawthorne near Pickering. The remains of Wade's Causeway, a Roman military road, are exposed at Wheeldale Moor. In addition there is a wealth of religious memorials. Standing stone crosses of great antiquity with strange names like Fat Betty, Lilla and Ralph can be found all over the moor. There are ruins of Cistercian abbeys at Rievaulx and Byland, but the Benedictine monastery at Whitby has survived and there is a beautifully preserved Carthusian priory at Osmotherley. Many of the village and town names are of Norse or Saxon origin.

The landscape still bears the traces of mediaeval farming and, because man has cleared, burned and grazed

– in other words, managed – the land for three thousand years, the North York Moors have become Britain's largest expanse of heather-covered upland.

After the fall of the monasteries, industries developed and the towns grew and became prosperous. Farming was improved and the old methods were refined. The mediaeval longhouses were abandoned or given to estate workers. Sturdy stone farmhouses were built in their place, and dry stone walls were used to separate the fields. The people who lived on the moor continued to be the main influence on the shape and appearance of the land.

Farming remains the principal occupation on the moors, although the total number of farming employees has reduced significantly since the Second World War. Mixed farming, restricted to coastal areas and limited parts of the uplands, produces cereals and root crops, with dairy and beef cattle and a small number of sheep. Rearing sheep is the main activity on the high moors, and the grazing here is confined to the heather moor and the enclosed grassland owned by the farmer. Although sheep farming is still a hard life, the agricultural improvements on the high moors have led to better grazing, but there has been consequential loss of the traditional features of the countryside.

Changes in land use have been extensive and dramatic, particularly during the last thirty years. There has been a massive loss of moorland vegetation. In 1953 it constituted 49 per cent of the National Park and by 1986 it had been reduced to 35 per cent. Erosion of the moorland is not new. During times of national turmoil such as the Napoleonic Wars, fringes of the moor were cultivated to counteract food shortages. When the emergency had passed the land was abandoned and eventually returned to heather moorland. However, twentieth-century farming methods have, through the use of new fertilisers, chemicals and machinery, been able to 'reclaim' primary moorlands which have never before been farmed.

The modern farmer has done immense harm to the character of the North York Moors. Mechanisation has not simply reduced the work-force and the communities

Hole of Horcum

Near Lastingham/near Fylingdales

Near Castleton/near Goathland

Wade's Causeway, a Roman road

which the farm labourers sustained, it has resulted in brutal changes to the landscape. Woodland and hedgerows have disappeared, and wire fences have replaced the old stone walls. The constant use of chemicals has stimulated the harvest and the cash return on the land while at the same time destroying birds, insects and animals. The change from hay to silage has removed many species of wild flower and the insects which lived upon them. A chain built up over thousands of years has been snapped at a stroke.

Old agricultural buildings have often disappeared too, only to be replaced with corrugated iron sheds and intrusive, shiny steel silos. Intensive farming units are some of the worst examples and those used for poultry and pig rearing are amongst the ugliest. Intensive farming, with its attendant problems of effluent, disease and smell, is no longer confined to lowland farms and several examples can now be found on the Tabular Hills. The mass production of animals is a high-risk business and all too often the units degenerate into unsightly decay when the enterprise has failed.

Today about a quarter of the Park, mostly in the southeast, consists of forest, much of it coniferous and managed by the Forestry Commission. Since 1953 over 48 square miles of the Park have been lost to afforestation. The original plantations were established in the 1920s without consideration for the appearance of the countryside, the amenities of the local population or the wildlife which lived on the moor. The resulting drab, green, geometric shapes on the hills were condemned by all who saw them. Today, cooperation between the Park Authority and the Forestry Commission is good and the Government's recent commitment to protection of the English uplands from large scale conifer afforestation should protect the moors from further damage.

Five per cent of the Park is covered by deciduous woodland, much of it a relic of the original tree cover. It is dominated by oak and ash although there is a wide variety of trees in the Park and rich diversity of plants, birds and insects. Woodland management and tree planting schemes have begun to increase the percentage of deciduous trees and the consequential benefits they bring to the countryside.

Military activity continues to dominate a well-loved area of the Park. Eight thousand hectares of Fylingdales Moor is now used for training by the Army and the character of the moor has been devastated by the massive white Radar domes of the Ballistic Missile Early Warning System. These are to be replaced with an even uglier triangular structure.

There has been great concern about the loss of moorland in recent years. The decline in the numbers of grouse since 1930 was an indication to the Park Authority that all was not well. Although the reasons for this are not completely understood, it is thought that the responsibility lies with the lack of a programme of heather burning which has allowed the encroachment of bracken, together with disease and pollution, a consequent decline in the nutrient value of heather, and climatic change. Today there is a comprehensive moorland management programme involving the Park Authority, the Countryside Commission, landowners, scientists and Government bodies. Land is being deliberately protected because of its scenic or scientific value and nature reserves and conservation areas have been created. In 1977 the Park Authority introduced an upland management scheme to encourage farmers to retain the old traditional characteristics of the land and to prevent damage from tourism by installing gates and stiles.

In spite of the protection of National Park status, much of North Yorkshire's priceless moorland has been lost since 1953. CPRE has worked hard at national level to influence policy on land use and advise on the conservation of moorland and the excesses of modern farming. A new integrated farming scheme has been devised by the Park Authority to make the most of the new opportunities for environmentally-friendly farming. Although lack of money has severely restricted any real progress, there are signs that the erosion of the unique character of the moors is slowing down.

Goathland, 1975

Near Glaisdale/Low Baring near Rosedale Abbey

Rosedale Moor/near Hutton-le-Hole

The Norfolk Broads

DAN LEPARD (photographs on pages 174–5) is a newcomer to the intricacies of landscape work, having spent most of his commercial life in advertising and fashion photography. At twenty-three, he is the youngest photographer in the Legacy project and has brought a dramatic and refreshing approach to his vision of the Broads. His portfolio of work was shot during a grey week in January. 'I was very aware of the emptiness of the countryside and the air of depression in the local communities. Much of the employment is seasonal and concerned with tourism and in the winter months both the landscape and the workforce seem to have knocked off until the season starts again. I tried to express this sort of "dead" feeling in my photographs.'

MARTIN TRELAWNY (photographs on pages 151–71) is a Cornishman working in Kent. His appreciation of the country and his understanding of the importance of the principles of conservation grew during the time when he ran the photographic department at the National Trust. Today, he specialises in landscape photography and his skill is evident in the books on the English rural scene where his work has been featured.

His love of East Anglia dates from his childhood, much of which was spent in Suffolk. 'The family used to escape at weekends to a little shack on the river near Womack Dyke in Suffolk. I returned there during the Legacy project and I was surprised at how much has been preserved. But the problem with the Broads is not just the pressure created by huge numbers of tourists, it is the dreadful, unsympathetic architecture which has been allowed in many of the old villages.'

ON 15 MARCH 1988, the Norfolk and Suffolk Broads Act was given the Royal assent. Forty-four years earlier a report by John Dower, 'Father of the National Parks', had recommended that the Broads should be dealt with by special legislation to meet its particular needs, combining national and local action. The passing of the act marked the end of a long fight by CPRE and others to enforce protection for a unique landscape.

The Hobhouse Committee had recommended that the Broads should become a National Park as long ago as 1947. For over forty years those who cared for this corner of East Anglia watched with mounting concern as its ecological decline continued. The Broads are internationally important and the environmental map of the area is liberally sprinkled with nature reserves and Sites of Special Scientific Interest. The Broads and marshes in the area of the Bure and Upper Thurne rivers were recognised in the 1971 Ramsar International Wetlands Convention.

However, the actions of the Ministry of Agriculture and the local water authority appeared to conspire against the flower-rich water-meadows, and no political initiative was forthcoming until the late 1970s. The Countryside Commission then set up a non-statutory Broads Authority whose staff and resources, though tiny, were able to take the first steps towards identifying the underlying causes of the problems and promoting solutions. Then in 1981 CPRE launched a campaign to stop the ploughing up of Halvergate Marshes for cereal production and the Broads were firmly on the political agenda.

The marshes were originally mud flats which were partially drained in the seventeenth century and the water level controlled by a system of wind pumps. Low-intensity grazing is fundamental to their character. The grassland attracts a wide variety of birds to nest and feed, and contributes to the traditional, visual character of the Broads. Arable farming can only be achieved by the drainage and fertilising of the marshes.

Arable fields are a hostile environment for many Broadland species of fauna and flora. The modern drainage of wetlands requires deep dykes and unsightly

Once part of the network of commercial waterways carrying corn, coal and timber, the Norfolk Broads by the 1930s were sailed mainly by pleasure boats. Traffic was more modest than it has now become, and the boats were light dinghies and yachts.

Traditional open grazing marshes at Halvergate have survived the passage of six decades, albeit in a reduced state

CPRE successfully campaigned to preserve Halvergate Marshes

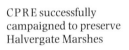

The land around the
skeleton windpump at How
Hill was the focus of the
campaign in the early
1980s to reform
agricultural policy

The reed harvest at
Salhouse

pumping stations. Between 1965 and 1980 around one-third of the area's marshland had been converted to crops because farmers were encouraged by a system of grants for drainage and subsidies to convert their land for the production of unwanted grain – grain which headed rapidly into EEC intervention stores. Following the 1981 Wildlife and Countryside Act, the Broads Authority would have had to compensate farmers for lost profits if they did not drain their land, and it did not have this sort of money. The CPRE campaign for Halvergate resulted in a rapid awakening of public concern about the loss of such landscapes to intensive farming, and helped encourage the Ministry of Agriculture and the Countryside Commission to introduce the Broads grazing marsh conservation scheme, which preserved the marshes by paying farmers to keep the land for their livestock.

The focus on Halvergate Marshes brought renewed attention to the whole Broads area, and led the Nature Conservancy Council and the Countryside Commission to issue a statement pointing out that unless immediate action was taken the Broads would be damaged beyond repair. Then in 1986 the Government announced in a letter to CPRE that it would bring the Broads Bill before Parliament. The Broads Act of 1988, while not being as tough as CPRE urged, enshrines the principles of sound conservation management and, at the same time, accommodates commercial demands on the rivers. It represents a profound environmental challenge.

The area of Norfolk and North Suffolk covered by the Broads incorporates a complex of closely related but varied landscapes and habitats. The three main rivers running through the region, the Ant, the Bure and the Yare, all sustained by numerous tributaries, drain 2,800 square miles through their estuaries into the North Sea.

The Broads themselves are man-made, the result of extensive peat extraction during the Middle Ages. The peat was used locally and transported by barge to the old cathedral city of Norwich where it was used as fuel. The workings were abandoned after a rise in sea level flooded the pits in the fourteenth century. It was not until 1950 that archaeologists agreed that these huge holes could have been created by excavation. The scale of the work was so enormous, it was difficult to accept that men and the primitive methods which they had at their disposal could have been responsible for such a major change to the landscape.

The pattern of lakes and rivers has changed constantly since the pits were first dug. The more shallow lagoons gradually became choked with sediment and vegetation, before silting up and becoming grazing farmland. Victorian tythe maps show a total area of 3,000 acres of lakeland while an aerial survey in 1980 showed that this had shrunk by about half. Some of the pits excavated by our ancestors were as deep as 3 yards while others dug after the water level began to rise were little more than shallow ponds.

In the upper reaches of the principal rivers, the fen and the Carr woodland (a dense, overgrown type of tree cover which is rich in animal and plant life) give an enclosed feel to the countryside. This changes to open, level fen as the rivers mature although the view from the water is sometimes blocked by thick reed beds and flood walls.

The charm and beauty of the Norfolk Broads was eloquently described by Arthur Ransome who brought to life the magic of a corner of England where boats sailed across quiet waters, where the Marsh Harrier slipped silently through the skies, where bitterns nested and where the otter was occasionally seen. The Norfolk rivers were busy with commerce and local industry. Ransome describes the staithes at Potter Heigham and Acle and writes about the wherries sailing down to Lowestoft between banks of reed.

But that was in the years immediately before the Second World War. Since those enchanted days the waterways have suffered badly. In addition to the loss of grazing marshland to arable agriculture, there has been progressive erosion of the river banks as a result of the wash from flotillas of tourist boats, as well as the disappearance of many miles of the dense reed buffers. Angling is a popular sport on the Broads and has led to serious damage to the

The harvesting of willows, osiers and reeds, used for thatching and all kinds of wickerwork, made a valuable contribution to the local economy

Opposite A flat-bottomed boat with bundles of reed being rowed upstream, Salhouse, January 1937

Barton Broad

The sand bank at Horsey was breached in the great storm of 1938

river bank vegetation through the trampling of reed beds and boats being illegally moored. Most important of all, there has been wholesale loss of the varied plant life. Many of the special natural habitats which have given character to the Broads have disappeared, choked to death as a result of changes in the level of chemical pollution in the water.

In those idyllic pre-war days when Ransome published *Coot Club* and *The Big Six*, the problems of pollution were never considered. The Broads were a healthy, stress-free haven where traffic jams caused by long queues of nose-to-tail boats were impossible to contemplate. Those who had the means, desire or wherewithal to spend their free time here did so in small numbers and caused little concern. The delicate balance between agriculture, tourism, commercial exploitation and domestic development remained largely intact.

The destruction of the natural purity of the water was rapid. Until the turn of the century, the rivers and lakes were sparkling and clear. Fifty years later the same waterways were so clogged with vegetation that channels had to be cut through them.

Nutrient levels in the water rose quickly in the post-war years. They came from the nitrates used in agricultural fertilisers and the phosphates from sewage treatment. The effect on plant life was almost instantaneous and, as more sewage from the growing local population was discharged into the water, the river vegetation grew luxuriously and in abundance.

By the 1960s the water had become contaminated with algae which caused discolouration and prevented sunlight from reaching below the surface. This created a chain reaction destroying the plants and a range of aquatic animals which relied on them. Wildfowl, deprived of their normal food, turned to young reed shoots and this in turn resulted in the loss of the reed buffer and encouraged erosion on the banks. The erosion created sediment which fell into the water, silting up the rivers and Broads.

Today, the state of the waterways varies considerably.

Salhouse, Norfolk

Opposite, top Horsey: sand hills where Broads and sea almost meet; *bottom* The River Thurne, 1940s

Boardman's Mill, How Hill, and the
adjacent land, is now owned by the
Broads Authority, which is running it as
a model Broad

Opposite The peace and charm of the
Broads still survives

Drainage mill, Hickling

Opposite Barton Broad

Broads such as Blackfleet, Upton and Brundall Gardens, which are separated from farming by unexploited fen, are spared the effect of nitrate 'run off' and sewage or livestock effluent. They are consequently clear and support flourishing plant and animal life. Phosphate levels in these unfortunately limited areas are around 20 microgrammes per litre. At the other end of the scale in Broads where attempts at conservation have until now been hindered by the lack of any statutory authority, the water is filthy. Propellers have stirred up the mud, nitrates have encouraged the growth of algae, other plant life is dead and the phosphate level has been pushed up to 1,000 microgrammes per litre. When the contrast in water purity is as marked as this, it means that the reasons can be monitored with accuracy and solutions can be found.

A number of experimental conservation programmes have begun to record successes. The badly silted Cockshoot Broad was separated from the polluted waters of the River Bure in 1982. Over 1 million cubic feet of sediment was then removed and nutrients in the water were immediately reduced. Plant life has gradually returned to the Broad and the water has improved in clarity. River bank erosion has been halted in many areas and the toes of the banks have been strengthened with nylon mesh which encourages vigorous reed growth and prevents erosion of the banks below water level. Phosphorus reduction programmes have been initiated in the River Bure and the River Ant. Similar work has also been started in Barton Broad, where artificial plants have been used as a means of attracting plankton and improving the clarity of the water.

The degeneration of the Broads is not simply an environmental problem – it has acquired a moral and economic significance. The escalating costs of repair and renewal have meant that unless money is made quickly available, the consequences for holiday makers, local industries, residents, farmers and those who love the Broads will be catastrophic.

Since the Broads Bill became law, the Broads Authority

has become a statutory body with representation from local authorities, the Countryside Commission, Anglian Water and the Great Yarmouth Port and Haven Commissioners. It is responsible for creating and instituting policies to direct long-term investment towards restoration through sound scientific principles.

CPRE campaigned for many years for legislation which will ensure that the fragile environment of the Broadlands is protected by status comparable with that of National Parks. On top of the immediate demands of a rare and delicately balanced ecology which has been allowed to deteriorate, the new Authority will have to deal with the problems created by the privatisation of water, improve water quality throughout the Broads, preserve the landscape and protect the land itself as the threat of sea level rises becomes more apparent. It will also be expected to encourage the Government to allocate sufficient resources for the vital job it has to do. It deserves our good wishes.

Intensive farming has overtaken much of the Norfolk landscape

Picture Credits

Jonathan Cape and CPRE would like to thank the following for their kind permission to reproduce the archive photographs: Beamish North of England Open Air Museum – pp. 17 top and bottom, 20, 21, 24 top and bottom, 25; Exmoor Society – pp. 121 top and bottom, 124; Hulton-Deutsch – pp. 116, 137, 168 top and bottom, 169, 173; Institute of Agricultural History, Reading University – pp. 29 top and bottom, 32, 33, 36, 37, 40 top and bottom, 41, 45 top and bottom, 48, 49, 52, 53 top and bottom, 56, 57, 61 top, 64 top and bottom, 65, 68 top and bottom, 69, 72 top and bottom, 73, 77 bottom, 80 top, 84, 85, 112, 117, 133 top and bottom, 136 top and bottom, 140, 141, 144 top and bottom, 145, 164, 165; Keystone Collection – pp. 81 bottom, 103 top and bottom; North Yorkshire County Library – pp. 149, 152, 153, 156, 157; Open Spaces Society – p. 172; Sheffield and Peak District (CPRE) Branch – pp. 89 top and bottom, 92, 93, 96 top and bottom, 97, 100, 101; *The Times* – pp. 61 bottom, 81 top, 109, 113, 125, 161; Topham Picture Library – pp. 77 top, 80 bottom; West Country Studies Centre – p. 108 top and bottom.

Index

Entries in bold type indicate photographs; brackets
indicate chapters in which places are mentioned